Fighting for Change

Black Social Workers
in Nova Scotia

Edited by
Wanda Thomas Bernard

Pottersfield Press, Lawrencetown Beach, Nova Scotia

Library and Archives Canada Cataloguing in Publication

Fighting for change : Black social workers in Nova Scotia / Wanda Thomas Bernard, editor.

ISBN 1-895900-80-8

1. Black Canadian social workers--Nova Scotia. I. Bernard, Wanda Thomas

HV109.N64F53 2006   361.3'092'3960716   C2006-900156-1

Pottersfield Press acknowledges the ongoing support of The Canada Council for the Arts, and the financial support of the Government of Canada through the Book Publishing Industry Development Program for our publishing activities. We also acknowledge the support of the Nova Scotia Department of Tourism, Culture and Heritage.

Cover design: Gail LeBlanc

Pottersfield Press
83 Leslie Road
East Lawrencetown
Nova Scotia, Canada, B2Z 1P8
Website: www.pottersfieldpress.com
To order, phone 1-800-NIMBUS9 (1-800-646-2879)
Printed in Canada

Canada Council   Conseil des Arts
for the Arts   du Canada

Canadä

NOVA SCOTIA
Tourism, Culture and Heritage

This book is dedicated to my mother,

Marguerite Thomas Parent

(April 26, 1926 – October 21, 2005),

who taught me through her lived experience

that "even a hard life can be wonderful."

Table of Contents

Section Four:
Making Institutional Change

Acknowledgements

This book is part of a long arduous journey, and many people have helped to make it a reality. I would like to thank all the contributors to the book for taking time, and risks, to write their stories, and to share their experiences. They do so with a desire and expectation that you, the readers, will be positively impacted by what is written here.

Special thanks and gratitude need to be expressed to all members of the Association of Black Social Workers (ABSW), which is the foundation on which this work is built, and to activist and artist David Woods, who inspired us to "tell the story" of the Black social workers in Nova Scotia.

I am grateful to Lesley Choyce and his team at Pottersfield Press for their diligent work on the manuscript. In addition, I thank Christie Ezurike, Bumni Oyinsan, Pauline Byard and Laura Swain for their assistance with the manuscript.

I have been privileged to have had many mentors, role models and wonderful ancestors, on whose shoulders I climb, and who taught me to lift as I climb, as I have fought for change. I am grateful to each one, too numerous to name here, for their many gifts to me over the years. Their spirits are in this book and in the work of ABSW.

Finally, I wish to thank my partner, George Bernard, for his unwavering support of every project I take on, and to my amazing family, who have loved and sustained me forever.

Introduction

Wanda Thomas Bernard

In May, 1979, I joined three women to organize a Halifax chapter of the Association of Black Social Workers (see Chapter 2), and I have been an active member of the group since then. The work of ABSW was recognized nationally on June 10, 2005, when I was awarded membership in the Order of Canada by Governor General Adrienne Clarkson. The citation reads:

An educator, scholar and social work practitioner, Wanda Thomas Bernard is a model of tolerance, understanding and compassion. Director of the Maritime School of Social Work at Dalhousie University, she is highly regarded for addressing racial and cultural diversity in social work education and in the community. She is a thoughtful leader who has generously shared her expertise in family and social development with local, provincial and national organizations, notably as a founding member of the Association of Black Social Workers. With courage and integrity, she has empowered the community at large to combat racism throughout all levels of society.

As I accepted this prestigious award, I noted that it was not mine alone, but was shared with the people with whom I had worked over the years. The editing of this book is another part of the journey begun so many years ago: a journey of racism and oppression; a journey marked by courage, resilience and empowerment. The telling of these stories of Black social workers in Halifax is another act of resistance. Using authoethnography, each author in this book tells her story in a way which creates a conversation with the reader about Black social workers who are breaking barriers and fighting for change for themselves as workers and for their clients and communities. They tell their stories about gaining entry to social work education and their experiences in social work. They also reflect on the change strategies that made a difference in their lives and the lives of the people they work with.

Using Africentric theory, the authors here explore the meanings of their struggles in order to provoke readers to enter the worlds of Black social workers and to reflect critically on their experiences. (By Africentric we mean centred on the African experience. The concept of Africentricity is explored in detail in Chapter 15.)

The book is divided into four parts. Section One tells the story of Black social workers' entry into the profession in Nova Scotia, and chronicles the poignant story of the life and eventual death of the Association of Black Social Workers (ABSW) in Montreal, from where the Halifax chapter was formed in 1979. Highlights of the successes and challenges faced by ABSW in Halifax are presented in Chapter 3. In Section Two, seasoned Black social workers, each a trailblazer in her own right, tell their stories of studying social work and beginning practice in Halifax in the late 1970s to early 1990s.

Section Three spotlights current students who relate stories of their reasons for entering the social work profession, and the barriers they face as they pursue their future career goals. The fourth section focuses on Africentric perspectives and presents some findings from exploratory research based on an Africentric perspective. Section Four discusses the common themes that emerge through each of the stories.

This anthology illustrates, through first voice accounts, the everyday realities and, as Essed (1991) says, "everyday racism" experienced by these social workers. They have had to overcome many struggles to survive and succeed, and the struggle and journey continues. As you read each story, and the story of ABSW, we invite you to imagine the struggle, then imagine the resistance, and finally, imagine what you can do to join the fight for change.

References

Essed, P. (1991). *Understanding everyday racism: An interdisciplinary theory*. Newbury Park, CA: Sage Publications.

Section One:

Beginnings

Chapter 1

The National Association of Black Social Workers Comes to Montreal

Diane C. Jacobs, PhD

From the mid 1970s through the 1990s, various social service agencies providing services to English-speaking and Jewish communities amalgamated into one institution due to directives from the Quebec government. That organization is now known as Batshaw Youth and Family Centres. In the late 1970s Black workers in various divisions of Batshaw voiced concerns regarding services to and policies about Black families. Several Black community organizations such as the Jamaican Association and the Black Community Council of Quebec (BCCQ) also began to express some of the same concerns.

To put things into context, it should be noted that the concerns raised about services to Black children and families were not unique to Batshaw. Some of the same issues were also raised by Haitian social workers employed by social service centres providing services to French-speaking children and families. This should come as no surprise because as persons of colour, and whether our mother tongue was French or English, we were products of the same race-conscious and racist society. And expanding the social context even further, social workers from various cultural groups in the United States were beginning to question the profession's use of dominant culture treatment methodologies. Several of our professional social work journals began to dedicate entire issues to particular cultural groups such as First Nations, African American and Hispanic communities.

I focus on Batshaw because that is where most English-speaking Black social workers were employed. The major concern we and Black community organizations identified was the overrepresentation of Black children in care of a child welfare system, given their numbers in the broader community. Black front-line workers in the mid '70s identified this issue as one needing to be addressed in a systemic way by those in a position to bring about change – the organizational senior managers.

A related concern was that some Black children continued to be placed in white foster homes despite the belief of many Black Canadians that they best be socialized to our racist society by Black parental figures. Our position was that placement in a culturally congruent home should be the first option. However, if such a placement was not available, no child should be deprived of a foster or adoptive home. Foster or adoptive parents committed to exposing the children to their communities of origin, while the agency involved worked to increase the number of culturally congruent foster homes.

There was a related concern that some Black children were being placed in remote communities where they seldom saw another Black person and were cut off from their own culture. This also made it difficult for some financially strapped parents to visit their children. In addition, there were still some foster parents who were not knowledgeable about caring for the skin and hair of Black foster children. Coupled with this was the difficulty in getting the organization to provide Black hair and skin care products for Black children in reception centres. To some this seemed like a trivial issue. However, without these cultural products children's self-esteem could be adversely affected. Laurie (a pseudonym) was an example of a child who grew up with cultural confusion. She was placed from birth with white foster parents. This was meant to be a short-term placement since Laurie had been relinquished for adoption at birth. But for some inexplicable reason Laurie was never adopted. Laurie was biracial (Black/white) and came to the agency when she was in her mid-twenties wanting to know a little about her "Black side." Laurie's poignant words best explain how she grew up with cultural confusion:

"I knew my white side but my foster parents would get very upset when I tried to talk to them about my Black side. So eventually I stopped asking. All I knew was that my mother was white and my father was Black. I would have liked to know where my mother was from and why she gave me up. I would have liked to know where my father was from and what his customs were. But my whole childhood I never saw another Black face other than what I saw in the mirror every morning and that was very painful.

"I had all these little white friends in elementary school. But I didn't understand what it meant when some kids started calling me nigger. My foster mother told me to just ignore those kids and how sticks and stones might break my bones but names would never hurt me. I loved my parents dearly but that answer did not begin to take away my pain.

"So here I was in the middle of nowhere, in the country. And suddenly in high school I was no longer invited to parties by the girls and boys I used to associate with. They were now forbidden by their parents to have anything to do with me. I mean, come on! This was my adolescence. It was supposed to be the best part of my life. Instead I was very lonely and I often asked myself what was there so awful about me that my parents (biological parents) did this to me.

"Later in high school I joined the basketball team. It was great because I got to play against teams in large cities like Montreal. I remember I used to get so excited when I saw Black girls on the other team. I wanted to run up to them and hug them. But then

I didn't know how to speak English – I lived in a totally French community. And I knew nothing about Black culture."

Laurie wanted to find out as much about her background as possible and had immersed herself in the Black community so that her young sons would not grow up with the cultural cut-off she had experienced. So she contacted the agency which placed her. Since she had never been adopted, Laurie was able to obtain non-identifying information from her file.

In the mid 1970s we were also concerned that there were so few Black social workers in proportion to the Black clientele. This had implications for the provision of culturally sensitive services. Similarly, we were concerned about the need for more Black foster/adoptive resource workers in order to recruit more culturally congruent homes.

In 1976 Black workers from all divisions of Batshaw were invited to a meeting with Bill Duncan, a Black senior manager, to discuss our feelings about the provision of social services to Black children and families. We shared our concerns about the need for services to be more culturally sensitive. In the end, Bill proposed organizing a chapter of the United States-based National Association of Black Social Workers (NABSW) in Montreal as a means of addressing some of our collective concerns. This proposal was unanimously agreed upon by those present. Unfortunately, before we could act, Bill relocated.

In 1977 Enid Dixon and I attended the annual NABSW conference. After giving feedback to various colleagues in the organization on the conference and the NABSW, Enid and I were encouraged to take leadership in organizing a chapter. So with the assistance of many of our colleagues within Batshaw and in the Black community at large, we established the Montreal chapter of the National Association of Black Social Workers. The late Cenie Williams (a founding member of the US organization and then on the NABSW national executive) and executive members from NABSW in Albany, New York, met with us in Montreal to get the group started. However, after about a year we decided to establish our own organization, because of cultural differences with the American group and membership expenses. We obtained a national charter as the Association of Black Social Workers of Canada (ABSW). We had a large membership who gave of their time and expertise in many ways. There was a loyal circle of twelve or so who attended the monthly meetings of the Association of Black Social Workers. Others were called upon to use their skills (for example, give a workshop), or they would help behind the scenes by contacting the right person to give us a donation or by assisting in whatever ways possible to keep the organization going.

What were some of the things we did as an organization? We had a weekend conference at Dawson CEGEP (junior college) featuring Mary Bailey, a social worker who used the reevaluation co-therapy approach. We had Saturday events for Black children placed in white foster homes so they could socialize with other Black children. We had Halloween and Christmas parties for Black children in residential settings. We had two Dawson CEGEP students do their field placements at Northmount High School, a high school that the system basically gave up on until Principal Gwen Lord turned it around. These two students assisted Ms. Lord in her outreach program to the students' parents and the broader community.

Finally, a group of Montreal NABSW members and supporters attended a regional NABSW conference in upstate New York. One of the supporters, Tommy Green, described the empowering experience: "I have extremely fine memories of the Black Social Workers Association and our great trip to Buffalo. It was this organization to which I owe my serious awareness of my origins. That trip allowed me to attend workshops on Black history and awareness. I often say (when asked to speak during Black Awareness Month) that having attended that conference, my sense of identity was so well developed. My memories of NABSW are extremely vivid and that must have been one of the most fruitful and beneficial events of my Black life. Ever since then when anyone asks what are my origins I proudly say that I am Afro-Canadian."

Several of our members relocated, while others found themselves overwhelmed with other responsibilities. The end result was that the same small nucleus of Black social workers who did most of the work got tired and reluctantly we disbanded the association. Individual members and supporters continued to advocate for Black clients – internally within Batshaw. In a non-confrontational manner, NABSW workers began to talk with individual managers about the need to deliver more culturally sensitive practice. A dialogue between Black social workers began to develop, resulting in a serious look at services to Black clients. The organization initially took baby steps, such as ensuring a Black worker attended placement conferences where decisions about Black children were being made. Later, the Multicultural Multiracial Committee was developed and examined issues such as placement conference policies and staff development on culturally sensitive practice. Eventually, after evaluation of Batshaw by an external evaluator, the Board of Directors acknowledged its institutional racism, and cultural sensitivity training became mandatory for all employees from front-line workers and support staff to senior management. NABSW doesn't presume to take credit for this. However, it did provide the spark leading to Batshaw's self-examination.

At about the same time that NABSW was winding down, a former NABSW social work intern, Maxene Sheppard, was returning to her native Nova Scotia. On behalf of Black social workers in Nova Scotia facing similar issues regarding Black clients, Maxene requested permission to transfer the organizational charter there. The Montreal organization was pleased to see the movement continue.

Chapter 2

Four Journeys – One Vision:
ABSW Comes to Halifax

Wanda Thomas Bernard
& Barbara Hamilton-Hinch

Below are the stories of the four founding members of ABSW in Halifax, Nova Scotia, – Maxene Prevost Sheppard, Frances Mills Clements, Althea Tolliver, and Dr. Wanda Thomas Bernard – relating what brought them into the human service field. These are followed by their collective vision for ABSW and the provision of social work for African Nova Scotian clients and communities. The chapter concludes with their lessons for the next generation.

Maxene Prevost Sheppard

Maxene was born in Newport, Nova Scotia, in 1931, the youngest of seventeen children. Her family later moved to Halifax, where she graduated from Queen Elizabeth High School. She married Edward Sheppard shortly after graduation and moved to Truro, Nova Scotia. After struggling and fighting racism in Nova Scotia, while trying to start their lives as a couple, they set off for greener pastures and moved to Montreal. Maxene and Ed remained in Montreal for twenty-five years, raised their three children, and moved back to Halifax in 1977 to be closer to family members.

An active homemaker and community activist until her children were older, Maxene returned to school later in life to pursue a degree, an opportunity denied her in Halifax because of segregation and racism. She graduated with a degree in Family Life Studies from College Marie Victorian in Montreal in 1976. During her four years of studies Maxene first heard of ABSW. Completing her initial placement at the Children Service Centre, Maxene had an opportunity to work with a lot of Black families being served by that agency. Many of them were teenage immigrants who were being reunited with their parents following separation due to their immigration process. Many of the parents came first and sent for their children once they were established in Canada.

In the final year of her program Maxene worked for the Association of Black Social Workers under the supervision of Diane Jacobs, who had formed the organization in Montreal. Maxene worked as a field worker for ABSW, doing individual work with Black youth in the high schools. She describes this work as her most rewarding, and yet most frustrating. It was rewarding because of the direct contact with the youth and the opportunity to help them address the issues in their lives. However, it was also challenging because of witnessing everyday racism, and the lack of responsiveness on the part of white social workers and educators who questioned the need of her services and the program ABSW offered.

Maxene's telling of one experience is illuminating: "I had so many different challenging experiences working in the various schools in Montreal. I had to deal with the word nigger being written on walls and the administration not doing anything about it for weeks. As much as it bothered me and I wanted to do something about it, the students in the school were my main concern and I did not want to give the administration a reason to remove the Association of Black Social Workers from the school. I felt the

Black students needed me, and I was going to do all I could do to make sure they received the same level of education and support as any student."

Although the work was difficult, it was tough for Maxene to leave those students behind, as she prepared to return to Halifax with her family. As she says, "I did everything that I could to help the children try to fit in and feel like a part of society because there was little if anything that gave them a sense of security. Part of me wanted to stay there and work with them, to give them a sense of belonging in this alienating society . . . and leaving those students behind was extremely difficult."

It was then that Montreal's loss became Halifax's gain, as she promised and made a deep commitment to Diane Jacobs that she would start a chapter of ABSW in Halifax, having no real sense of how she would even begin to do that. And that seed called ASBW was planted in Halifax.

Frances Mills Clements

Frances was born and raised in Truro, Nova Scotia, and moved to Halifax when she married her first husband. Together they raised a daughter, until Frances became a young widow. Frances continued to live in Halifax, and was active in church and community leadership roles. This volunteerism eventually led to full-time employment with the Black United Front (BUF) as their Prison Liaison Worker, a position she held for twenty years prior to retirement. She continued her community activism work post-retirement, and moved to Bridgetown, Nova Scotia, where her second husband was originally from. Now widowed for a second time, Frances continues to be a community leader, activist and volunteer. She was the first Black municipal councillor to be elected in Bridgetown.

Frances says that her work in the prisons was most fulfilling, even though it was hard work. She says, "I saw a lot of positive things happen during my time working in the prison. There was one young fellow who I thought would be in prison for the rest of his life because of the crime he committed. However, after visiting

him on a regular basis and listening to him I was able to understand his situation better. Our communication was very effective
and within three years of my regular visits he was released from
prison. The fact he was released in three years made me feel a
sense of accomplishment."

Frances goes on to say that another highlight of her career was
being a part of the formation of ABSW. She indicates that this
enabled her to work in other areas outside of prison liaison work,
such as with the Children's Aid Society, and the opportunity to
engage in prevention work was very empowering. Frances says, "As
the ABSW became stronger and more involved in the communities,
many of the children who had white social workers would often
tell the Black social workers about the abuse they experienced. I
can say that many of the white social workers did not understand
the needs of our Black children."

Frances' passion for justice for Black children in care and her
work with young Black men in prisons fueled her drive to be a part
of the emergence of ABSW.

Althea Tolliver

Althea was born and raised in East Preston, Nova Scotia, a small
rural segregated Black community. She and her husband James live
there today, where they raised their family of two children, and
now enjoy the blessings of their four grandchildren. Althea says
that being part of a loving family, with parents who were socially
conscious, gave her a foundation for helping others. She vividly
recalls that "growing up in a small community, everybody kind of
looked after each other. And even before I knew what the words
social work meant, I guess, or even knew what a Safe House was,
our home was always a Safe House. I can think of a number of
people both young and old that came to our door in need, whether
it was for food or fleeing spousal abuse, or whatever was going on.
. . . [Many] people would confide in my mom or my dad, and
young people would come late at night."

Althea has worked in social work or the human service field for the last thirty years, and is currently the Childcare Director at the Nova Scotia Home for Colored Children. She began her career working in Mulgrave and Pugwash, Nova Scotia, as part of her Human Services diploma course, which eventually led her to go into social work. She is a graduate of the Dalhousie School of Social Work. While a student she completed her first field placement at the Nova Scotia Home for Colored Children. Although she says she thoroughly enjoyed her work at the Home, she was concerned about the evidence of systemic racism that was so visible to her. For example, Althea says that at the time, "All the social workers were white, and the clients were Black, and the staff were Black, but the decisions at the Home were made by the social workers in those days. I decided that I wanted to be one of those people who was in the decision-making role and making decisions about our kids."

In addition to working at the Nova Scotia Home, Althea is an active church and community leader in East Preston and has a passion for the maintenance of the human rights and dignity for all in society, which underpins her decision to become a founding member of ABSW.

Wanda Thomas Bernard

Wanda is also from East Preston, a graduate of a segregated elementary school. She and her older sister Valerie were two of the first three members of their community to have the opportunity to attend university. The sixth of twelve children, Wanda learned early in life about issues of race, institutional racism, classism and sexism, and how these marginalize us. Her mother was widowed when the family was still very young, and Wanda witnessed at a young age the capacity of the human spirit to heal even in the face of intolerable injustices. As she indicates, "I also made a decision that I was not going to just be aware of social injustice, but that I was going to do something about it," and the seeds for a life of passion for social justice were sown.

After receiving a Bachelor's degree, Wanda went on to graduate studies in social work at Dalhousie University. She worked in
the mental health field for twelve years prior to taking a full-time
teaching position at the Dalhousie School of Social Work, where
she has been Director for the past five years. She was the first African Nova Scotian to be hired in a tenure-track position, with the
expectation that she would complete the course work towards a
PhD in the first seven years of her appointment. She says, "I actually completed the PhD in my sixth year at the School, and recently
celebrated my sixteenth year at Dalhousie University. Given the
success of this hiring initiative, my experience of being mentored
through the academic process has been used by other departments
at Dalhousie and other programs across the country."

When asked to characterize her life's work in a few words,
Wanda says, "My work has been a journey where I have experienced much pain and marginalization at the intersection of race
and gender, but I have also had opportunities to challenge, to lead
by example, and to work with others for social justice. The invi-
tation to become a founding member of ABSW was a welcomed
opportunity to work with others who were also interested in fighting for social change. Maxene initially recruited me, and I recruited
Althea and Frances, and in 1979 we officially became the Halifax
Chapter of ABSW, with the Montreal group as our sponsors."

The Shared Vision

These four women were all community-minded, socially conscious
and politically astute women who saw a need in their community
and worked to address that need. The vision for ABSW began
with Maxene's promise to Diane Jacobs to help establish a branch
in Nova Scotia. She saw the positive impact it had in Montreal
and knew that together they could make a difference in Nova
Scotia. For each of the four women the number one priority was
her love for people, the love for African people, the love for the
community, the community at large, and the desire to bring about
change because of the injustices that they were all so painfully

aware of. They all felt that there were not enough Black social workers to deal with the issues relating to African Nova Scotian children. They felt that there was a need for this association, for a Black social work agency, so part of that vision was having their own Social Service Agency and they still hope to realize that vision some day.

They had a shared vision about changing the way that social services were being delivered to Black Nova Scotians. These four women started with a program that they had for Black children in white foster homes, so they had a vision of changing that whole process: first of all, changing the services those children were getting and then changing the policy that would put them in non-Black homes. They lobbied the provincial government and made changes to the Children and Family Services Act (see Chapter 3). They had a vision of racial matching, both in terms of the direct service and also in terms of support services and professional services, the counselling services. Their vision was also about really making changes in the School of Social Work in terms of curricula, student body, and faculty and staff.

Their primary vision was to get an association that would flourish, stay together, and bring in other workers as they moved along the journey. They wanted to have their own ABSW office and imagined that the Department of Community Services would use them as a tool to aid in the work that they were doing in the Black community. However, they were seen more as a threat. Wanda recalls that she was questioned after a meeting of the four members in her office and asked, "What are you guys planning, some sort of uprising?" From that day on the group met in each other's homes because it was perceived as unsafe to meet in their offices. Maxene recalls receiving a call from the provincial association of social workers (who were themselves a struggling organization at that time) challenging their use of the term "social workers" in the ABSW title. Despite these challenges, the four members continued to work towards systemic change in the delivery of social services to the Black community in Nova Scotia. Some of the highlights of their work over the past twenty-six years are featured in the next chapter.

With regards to the future these women still have a vision for what ABSW can do. Althea says her vision was to see ABSW have its own Social Services Agency. She suggests that there should be satellite offices set up to provide services to single parents similar to how there are satellite medical offices in some of our Black communities. Funding should be made available for such a service. These satellite offices would be administered by highly qualified social workers and our Black social worker students who have to do field placements could learn under Black social workers. There are many social workers who still operate under the colour blind theory and refuse to understand the difference that skin colour can make in relation to a service being provided. Althea also says, "There are some that are sensitive to the Black community but I don't think that is enough. We have a real need in our community. We have to strengthen our families and we have to listen to the community, reach out into the community and give the community some of the things they need and want."

Wanda says that "although we have had a number of successes, there is still much work to be done. ABSW needs to expand, especially in the rural areas. We need more Black social workers throughout the province, and we must encourage and support those who step up to administrative positions." Obviously, although they have been involved with ABSW for more than two decades, these founding members have not grown tired or weary. They have as much energy and enthusiasm for the work today as they had in 1979, and they are optimistic about the possibilities that lie ahead for the next generation of Black social workers in Nova Scotia.

Lessons for the Next Generation

The founding members have some encouraging words and lessons for the next generation. They realize the need for the next generation to be involved in ABSW and in their communities and the important role they can play as they continue the journey towards changing a system that marginalizes Black people. Althea says, "I would want the next generation to know who they are, to really be in tune with themselves and make sure they really have a love for the work." Frances says, "Lesson number one is get involved in your community and give back to the community that supports you even when you don't know you need support. I would also want the next generation to know the past in order to be better prepared for the future." That there needs to be recognition of the past struggles and victories is evident in Wanda's views: "I ask students to recognize that they stand on the shoulders of many who have gone before, who have paved a way, who have made the difference and that that's part of their current journey."

Finally, Frances speaks volumes when she says, "I think ABSW made a very big difference because it motivated more young people to go into the School of Social Work. Now we need you to give back to the community."

It is anticipated that through the voices of the women in this book, readers will experience a sense of hope as they share the founders' vision for a better future for the next generation, which is what they worked for in the humble beginnings. As Maxene so poignantly puts it, there is a lot for us to be proud of, even though there is still a lot more to be done: "Strange as it might sound, one of the greatest sources of satisfaction dawned on me when Wanda Thomas Bernard was made a member of the Order of Canada [for her work on racism in social work]. It made me feel so proud and I am sometimes surprised that we have survived it all and remain in existence! I cannot help feeling proud when I think of all the young people who have dedicated themselves to ABSW over the years."

The work of the founding members of ABSW leaves a legacy of individual and community empowerment, working towards a vision of autonomy and social justice for Black people and other marginalized groups. They are strong Black women who were activists before they came into the social work field, and they continue to resist and challenge to effect change.

Chapter 3

The Association of Black Social Workers in Halifax: A Brief History

Candace Bernard Roker

The Helping Tradition of the African Nova Scotian Community

Although Black people in Nova Scotia have a long and significant history here, we have not had a fair or equitable representation in critical decision-making processes. African Nova Scotians have been poorer than the average white Nova Scotian, who in turn has been poorer than the average Canadian. We have lived with a special burden of racism and discrimination throughout our history in this province (Bernard 1986). This history has been fraught with separate laws and provisions for African Nova Scotians. Speaking about the legacy of the "poor houses" in Nova Scotia, Dr. Fred MacKinnon states that if you were poor, you could go to a poor house; however, you had to be white. Black people were not allowed to live in the poor houses because of segregation laws. Therefore, separate houses were established to accommodate poor Black people. Looking specifically at the provision of social services, and child welfare services in particular, the Black community had to establish its own informal and formal institutions. For example, the Nova Scotia Home for Colored Children (NSHCC) was established by James R. Johnston, under the auspices of the African United Baptist Association (AUBA) because of this need. Prior to the establishment of the Nova Scotia Home for Colored Children, the African Nova Scotian community looked after orphaned, abused or abandoned children through informal adoption. Furthermore, many families relied on support from extended family networks for assistance with the responsibility of child-rearing.

Systemic racism and marginalization from the mainstream have largely characterized our history and experience here. Systemic racism and discrimination in Nova Scotia have historically led to the underdevelopment and marginalization of African Nova Scotian communities. The evidence of this is visible in the high unemployment rates in all forty of these communities and the subsequent lack of development is a consequence. There is an underrepresentation of African Nova Scotians in decision-making positions in the province. There is also underrepresentation at the local, municipal, and federal levels. On the other hand, African Nova Scotians are overrepresented in mandated community services, as clients, and underrepresented as workers in these agencies. For example, the Black Learners Advisory Committee Report on Education (1994), *Redressing Inequality – Empowering Black Learners,* clearly illustrates the historical and current inequalities in the education system, and the impact of these on Black learners.

Systemic racism is reflected in hiring practices and the continual underrepresentation of African Nova Scotian residents in positions where they are making decisions that affect the well-being of the group. This is visible in our overrepresentation in those services, which are mandated, and our lack of involvement in more voluntary services. The Association of Black Social Workers (1988) and Barkley (1985) have documented that Black people make up a high percentage of social service caseloads in Child Welfare and

Corrections. However, few go for voluntary counselling services in family service or mental health agencies. There are few African Nova Scotian professionals working in these agencies as well. This marginalization from the mainstream could have adversely affected the survival of African Nova Scotian people. However, what we have experienced is positive survival, using very creative strategies. One survival strategy has been the helping tradition of African Nova Scotian people and communities. For example, the African United Baptist Association (AUBA) formed in 1854 as a way of communities coming together, for support fellowship and spiritual development. The Nova Scotia Home for Colored Children is one of the most public examples of the African Nova Scotian community taking care of its own.

In addition to the Church there are also a number of secular organizations that enable us to be connected locally, regionally, nationally and globally. However, the Church is the most long-standing community-owned-and-operated institution which has served as a site for spiritual growth, as well as leadership on social justice issues. We have also had strong support from family and community, which has helped individuals and families in need. Similar experiences have occurred with our neighbours to the south, where the development of African American families and communities has been largely characterized by a tradition of African Americans helping African Americans. The Church and family have been the most significant care providers. Many of the early interventions focused on racial betterment and racial uplift (Iglehart and Becerra 1996).

In 1980 in the United Kingdom, Black professionals established the Family Support Service, a Black self-help project with Black single mothers. It became a useful model for working non-oppressively and supportively with Black single mothers (Bryan, 1992, p. 82). This project worked with the strengths of the Black women who participated in the service, utilizing a holistic model of program delivery, which included the whole community. As for other Africans in the Diaspora, the helping tradition of African

Nova Scotians has been a powerful survival strategy and this tradition continues, although to a somewhat lesser degree.

Informal Social Work Happening in the Black Community

Early initiatives in community work included the development of social housing cooperative programs. Community development such as youth groups and local chapters of the Canadian Red Cross Society, the Nova Scotia Association for the Advancement of Colored People, and the National Black Coalition raised consciousness about inequitable treatment of African Nova Scotians and gave people a voice to address their concerns to government agencies.

The formation of the Black United Front (BUF) in the early 1960s, which emerged after the critical race consciousness following the Civil Rights Movement, was likely the first organized effort to bring much needed social services to the Black community. One of the founding members of ABSW in Halifax, Frances Mills Clements, was a community worker with BUF and she saw the formation of ABSW as a way of augmenting her work at BUF.

Early Beginnings: The Initial Formation of ABSW

As indicated in Chapter 2, four women formed ABSW in Halifax in 1979. Although one of their major priorities was increasing membership, this was not successful and they functioned with four members until 1984. The lack of membership was partly because there were few Black social workers graduating from the School of Social Work in the early 1980s (Bernard, MacDonald and Wien, 2005). As Lois Fairfax attests in Chapter 8, many social workers who were graduating were not able to find employment in Nova Scotia and therefore left the region for social work opportunities in other provinces. Furthermore, ABSW was viewed as a politicized organization and some Black social workers felt their employment security would be threatened if they participated in the organization (see Chapter 2).

Despite these challenges, the four founding members were able to effect change on many levels. The primary focus of ABSW was around Black youth in care, which is explored later in the chapter. However, other initiatives were undertaken. For example, ABSW initiated an employment program for young Black men and women who had dropped out of high school. The project was funded by Human Resources Development Canada and led to the creation of many employment opportunities for these youth and the eventual development of the Cultural Awareness Youth Group (CAYG) as a motivator to keep Black youth in school. The CAYG went on to develop groups in high schools province-wide.

Another initiative was creating awareness around health education for Black women and their families. ABSW joined the Women's Health Education Network and held a conference on Black women's health in Halifax in 1983.

From 1984 to 1988 the four members were inactive due to burnout. In 1988 the Department of Community Services released a report from a task force on services to families, and the ABSW founding members noted the absence of attention to Black families. This provided the impetus to reorganize ABSW, and the group has flourished since then. Other factors which led to the growth in membership included the increase of Black social work graduates from the Dalhousie School of Social Work. Initiatives such as the School of Social Work Affirmative Action Program and more employment opportunities for social workers in Nova Scotia helped to increase the number of Black social work graduates (Bernard, MacDonald and Wien, 2005).

The original goals of ABSW were:

to provide a structure and forum through which Black social workers and human service workers can exchange ideas, offer service and develop programs in the interest of the Black community and the community at large;

to work in cooperation with, to support, develop or sponsor community welfare projects and programs, which will serve the interest of the Black community and the community at large;

to examine, develop and support social work and community-based programs of direct service or assistance to individuals in the Black community (ABSW, Minutes from meeting, 1985).

The current members of ABSW are primarily fully employed social workers who work with the organization as volunteers as well as social work students and human service workers. ABSW acts as a support group for African Nova Scotian social workers, in addition to its function as an action-oriented community group. In 1999 ABSW received a national award from the Canadian Association of Social Workers in recognition of its contribution to the profession, some examples of which are discussed below. In 2005 one of the founding members, Dr. Wanda Thomas Bernard, was awarded membership in the Order of Canada, for her twenty-plus years of work on racism in social work in Canada, and was identified in the citation as a "founding member of ABSW."

On the Front Lines: ABSW Community Work

The creation of a position statement about the placement of Black and biracial children in white foster and adoptive homes is one example of ABSW's community advocacy in an effort to improve child welfare services. ABSW stated that "the Black child should grow in a safe, secure environment with parents who are able to transmit to that child a positive sense of culture, identity and well being" (ABSW, Position Statement, 1989).

The following is an excerpt from the position statement: "The Association of Black Social Workers oppose the child welfare practices of transracial adoption and the foster placement of Black children in white homes. The Association of Black Social Workers adheres to the position that Black children be placed in Black homes where they belong physically, psychologically and culturally in order that they receive a total sense of themselves and are free to develop to their fullest potential. In the adoption/fostering of a child of minority racial or minority ethnic heritage, in reviewing adoptive/foster placement, the court shall consider preference, and in determining appropriate adoption/foster home, the court shall give preferences, in the absence of good cause to the contrary to (a) a relative or relatives of the child, or if that would be detrimental to the child or a relative is not available, to (b) a family with the same racial or ethnic heritage as the child or if that is not feasible, to (c) a family of different racial or ethnic heritage from the child that is knowledgeable and appreciative of the child's racial or ethnic heritage and has on-going contact with others of the child's ethnic or racial background" (ABSW, 1989).

This statement led to the active involvement of ABSW in the development of the revised Children and Family Services Act in 1991, and the inclusion of a policy around the provision of culturally specific services for children and families as part of the Act. ABSW also assisted with cultural sensitivity and anti-racism training for staff of various child welfare agencies in the province as part of the implementation of the new Act. Currently, members from ABSW volunteer to provide training on working with African Nova Scotian families as part of the core training program for all new child welfare workers.

The position statement and subsequent changes to the Nova Scotia Children and Family Services Act have made an important contribution to the provision of child welfare services in the province. Child welfare workers and agencies now have the legislative responsibility to take racial and cultural issues into consideration when providing child welfare services, from the first point of entry in the system to service provision. Several years after the position statement was issued, workers continue to use it to make culturally specific case plans for Black and biracial children.

The following quotation from an ABSW member is illustrative of the ways in which the legislation is used to do more effective planning for cultural diversity in child welfare: "I was recently asked by a child welfare worker in a rural agency to do a consultation regarding placement options for a sibling group of four biracial children. I was impressed with the worker's strategy to build the consultation into the case planning for this family."

In addition to challenging child welfare agencies and criticizing their failure to locate Black foster and adoptive homes, ABSW mounted an active recruitment campaign to help make implementation of the Position Statement and the new child welfare policy a reality.

Recruitment of Black Foster and Adoptive Homes

ABSW has offered assistance to child welfare agencies and acted as a liaison with Black communities in the recruitment of Black foster and adoptive homes. In addition, they advocated for the placement of children in the Nova Scotia Home for Colored Children when a Black foster or adoptive home was not available for a Black child in care. ABSW participates in the training of all foster families, particularly around issues of race and racism.

ABSW established a recruitment campaign to help agencies find suitable homes for Black and biracial children in care. A poster was prepared for use in the campaign and sent to strategic locations. In addition, ABSW members visited local churches and Black organizations to create awareness of the need for Black families to provide culturally specific foster and adoption options for these children.

This initiative led to the hiring of Black social workers in various agencies in Nova Scotia to actively recruit, train and support Black foster and adoptive families. This work, however, is happening primarily in the urban areas and not in the rural areas of the province. Recruitment of Black foster and adoptive homes is a difficult task, as historically the African Nova Scotian community has not had a positive relationship with government agencies, particularly child welfare services. However, there is a long tradition of informal adoption in the African Nova Scotian community. The major task of the agencies and recruitment workers will be to bridge the historical interest in informal adoption with the current policies regarding fostering and adoption.

Summer Program for Black and Biracial Youth in Care

The goal of this program was to address issues of self-esteem and racism and to provide summer recreational opportunities. The program helped to enhance the personal and community empowerment of low-income Black families and children. Many of these children have gone on to higher education partly as a result of this early intervention. The Summer Program for Black and Biracial Youth in Care was targeted for those youth who were living in white foster and adoptive homes. It was designed to help the youth deal with issues of identity, culture, and experiences with racism. The program linked these youth with each other, and with other youth from the African Nova Scotian community.

The majority of the youth who were referred to the summer program were living in isolated rural communities. They were usually the only Black children in the community. In a number of cases there were a large number of Black and biracial foster children living in one foster home. In one home there was a family of six, and in another, a family of five. The children were not related by blood, but as the only Black children in the family and community, they developed strong familial bonds. Most of these children experienced racism and a lack of cultural sensitivity in their homes, schools and communities. Their white foster or adoptive parents were not prepared or adequately trained to raise these children for the harsh realities they would face in a race conscious and racist society (Bernard 1996).

The ABSW Summer Program provided workshops for the youth on basic topics such as hair and skin care. There were also lessons in African Nova Scotian and world history, and sessions on building self-esteem and positive racial identity. ABSW also provided seminars on dealing with racism and handling conflict.

An unanticipated outcome of the program was that it reunited sibling groups. Youth who were separated when they went into foster care, and who were unaware of the fact that they actually had siblings, were suddenly in contact with them. In addition, the links with other community youth developed into ongoing friendships and in some cases long-term relationships. This linking of Black and biracial youth to their birth communities afforded them opportunities to build extended family and kin relationships that remain important ties for them today.

Support Groups (Black and Biracial Adult Adoptees, and SEARCH – Support, Education and Appreciation of Race, Culture and Heritage)

ABSW members, who were also graduate social work students, established two support groups. The first group was for Black and biracial adults who were raised in white foster or adoption homes, without a connection to their community of birth or their culture. Prior to the late 1970s there was little public discourse about transracial adoptions or foster care and much of the literature in this area focused on the experiences of parents, with little attention paid to the experiences of children.

In 1989-90, an ABSW member conducted a qualitative study with Black adults on their experiences of being raised in white homes (Johnson 1991). As they listened to each other's stories in a focus group, the participants identified many shared experiences. This led to their interest in forming a support group. The support group was facilitated by ABSW. The group enabled them to connect with each other and to support each other as they journeyed through the development of their racial consciousness. They went through a process of grief and a reclaiming of their identity. Eventually the group members developed a strong and positive sense of themselves as people of African heritage, a heritage and culture that had been denied to them. The lessons learned from this group of adults who had survived transcultural placements were later used in the training of social workers. They also contributed to our understanding of the need to change child welfare policy to include issues of race, culture and religion in the provision of services.

The second support group, SEARCH (Support, Education and Appreciation of Race, Culture and Heritage), was organized by another ABSW member and social work graduate student as part of her research on the development of identity in biracial children (Marsman, 1993). The SEARCH group provided support, education, training and counselling services for white parents who were raising Black and biracial children. The group included birth, foster and adoptive parents, all of whom were white, mixed race couples or individuals (usually mothers), raising children of African heritage.

The SEARCH group enabled the parents to come together in a safe forum, to address how best to meet the needs of their children. The group also provided opportunities for the youth to come together to address issues that were important to them. Many of the youth were dealing with issues of racism that they had not been able to discuss with their parents. Additionally, the parents developed a heightened awareness and analysis of their role in effectively parenting their children to deal with the racism that they experienced. They also gained practical skills such as managing hair and skin care, how to access community resources, and the power of establishing networks in the community.

Anti-racism and Cultural Sensitivity Training for Social Workers

ABSW created a workshop for BSW students at the Dalhousie School of Social Work. The workshop encourages participants to critically examine their own power and privilege and to experience oppression first-hand during the exercise. The two-part workshop, which focuses on awareness, analysis and action, was delivered by a dyad of ABSW members to the Introduction to Social Work class each year and to students in the Master of Social Work Colloquium. Moreover, ABSW has presented this workshop to over fifty agencies and organizations throughout Nova Scotia and other parts of Canada.

The Racism Awareness Workshop has been evaluated on two occasions: once by ABSW itself and again by Kaireen Chaytor of Chaytor Educational Services. The goal in both these evaluations was to examine the long-term impact of the training program. In each instance we learned that although participants were often angry and upset immediately after the simulation exercise, many described it as the single most significant learning experience they had concerning racism and anti-racism. The follow up evaluations tracked students and practitioners who had participated in a workshop. Graduates of the Dalhousie School of Social Work stated that the ABSW exercise helped them to understand oppression far better than any reading, textbook or lecture. They went on to say that the experiential exercise touched them at the affective level, which helps give them the passion to engage in actions against racism in an ongoing way.

ABSW designed and delivered a series of seminars dealing with racism as a health issue for Black social workers and human service workers. This project was funded by the Community Health Board, and was hugely successful in helping Black social workers and human service workers in both identifying racism in their workplace, and implementing strategies to address and redress the race oppression.

Development of Educational Materials

Project Hope was created as an awareness and consciousness-raising project targeting the issue of HIV/AIDS in the African Nova Scotian community. This project worked with youth to help them develop awareness and action around this critical issue. The youth developed a play on HIV/AIDS, which they performed in the local junior high schools and in the community at large.

Voice of the People was a video project aimed at giving rise to first voice accounts of racism in Nova Scotia. This video is now used as a teaching aid in social work education at the Dalhousie School of Social Work.

A workshop using the video *HIStory: Reflections on the Black Father-Son Relationship* is a strategy designed by ABSW to get Black men talking about their role as fathers, other-fathers, community fathers and grandfathers, in supporting Black fatherhood as a critical component for healthy parenting in African-Canadian communities. The structured educational workshops and related video provide a meaningful learning model that builds the skills and capacities of those participating in the project while nurturing important community support connections. The long-term goal of the project is to address the incidence of youth crime in the community by teaching important social values, offering positive societal options, and encouraging healthy family parenting practices. Challenging the pervasive negative stereotyping of Black fathers, the workshop leaders share information about the success of the fatherhood workshop, and the lessons learned.

Linkage with Department of Community Services

Africentric Initiative Training Program

The Africentric Initiative Training Program for adoption and foster care workers in the Halifax Central region of Nova Scotia was designed to develop an awareness of the lived realities of African Nova Scotians and Africans in the Diaspora, to introduce skills needed in the use of Africentric assessments for custody and placement cases involving African Nova Scotian (Black) and biracial children, and to evaluate the assessment tool developed by Roker and Bernard.

The program, a pilot study for the Nova Scotia Department of Community Services Foster Care and Adoption Unit, was designed and facilitated by Dr. Bernard on behalf of the Association of Black Social Workers (ABSW). Twenty workers and supervisors participated in the training, which took place one half-day per month over an eight-month period. The training sessions consisted of seven modules, covering topics on Africentricity; historical and contemporary perspectives on African Nova Scotians and Africans in the Diaspora; the recruitment, training and ongoing support for adoptive and foster families; and use of the assessment tool. Presentations, a panel of former children in care, and exercises comprised the training modules. An evaluation was completed after each session, and a follow-up external evaluation was conducted one year after the final training session. The trainers simultaneously provided a program for foster care and adoptive parents on the specific needs of the African Nova Scotian and biracial children in their care.

Fee for Service Program

This program provides culturally specific services for African Nova Scotians involved with child welfare agencies as clients on a fee for service basis. Racism and poor treatment have characterized the experiences of African Canadians in the child welfare and other social service systems such as mental health.

Turner and Jones assert that "[t]he Black culture is sufficiently different from Euro-American culture, for misunderstanding of behavioral processes and functions to have occurred. This misunderstanding has resulted in problems in service delivery and treatment approaches" (Turner & Jones, 1982, p. 21). In addition, they state that "Black patients are likely to evaluate therapy outcomes as negative if they feel that the therapist cannot understand them or their culture or is not interested in their welfare" (Turner & Jones, 1982, p. 21).

African practitioners are aware of this history and understand the feelings of fear and animosity that may surface in the worker/ client relationship. Because of the history of racist service in the past, many families will appreciate and may feel more comfortable having culturally specific services. In addition, it can be frustrating for clients to have to educate workers about their race and culture.

Ongoing services provided by ABSW include counselling, assessments, youth support work, tutoring, case aid, access visits, parent support and advocacy work. These services are contracted with local child protection agencies. ABSW has one staff person and one member of the executive who run the fee for service program. Skilled members of the African Nova Scotian community are hired and trained by ABSW to provide services on a contractual basis based on referrals from agencies.

Linkage with Dalhousie School of Social Work

ABSW developed a strong liaison with the Dalhousie School of Social Work. In the past, they have been actively involved with the school's Committee on Racial and Ethnic Affairs, and have assisted the school with its efforts to increase diversity in all aspects of the school's work. ABSW has participated in recruitment of faculty, mentorship with students and curriculum development. Currently, a member of ABSW sits on the school's advisory committee, whose membership includes various community members.

Bursary for Black Social Work Students

ABSW offers two bursaries per year for students studying in undergraduate or graduate programs at the Dalhousie School of Social Work. Fundraising is organized by ABSW members and often includes community-based initiatives such as bowl-a-thons, silent auctions, raffles and other such activities. Criteria for the bursary is based on academic merit, financial need and community activism.

Linkage with Nova Scotia Association of Social Workers

ABSW has secured representation on the Nova Scotia Association of Social Workers Council. This enables the organization to work more collectively and collaboratively with all social workers in the province. Furthermore, it gives African Nova Scotians a voice, as ABSW is able to bring critical issues impacting the community to the attention of the larger community of social workers and to get support in dealing with these issues.

ABSW has held three major conferences: in 1989 Black Families: Strengthening Resources for the Future; in 1990 Cultural Sensitivity in Social Work Practice with Black Clients; and in 1997 Africentric Perspectives in Social Work Practice in conjunction with the Nova Scotia Association of Social Workers. These conferences have enabled ABSW to share their expertise with a wider audience of social workers and community members. They also have served as a bridge between social work organizations and the Black people and communities they serve. Despite these successes, however, these initiatives are not enough to maintain sustained systemic changes in the ways in which policies are developed and services are delivered.

Community Outreach

ABSW has a number of projects and initiatives that provide some form of community outreach. We are frequently asked to represent ABSW on local, provincial and national organizations, new initiatives, research and discussion of organizational and policy change. More locally, we organize a social tea each year during African Heritage Month to recognize, honour and celebrate seniors in the African Nova Scotian communities. This event is one of the ways in which ABSW gives back to the community and validates the helping tradition of our elders. The event includes entertainment, refreshments and a special tribute to local seniors. The event rotates and is held in one of the eight local Black churches in the Halifax Regional Municipality. We hold fundraisers for our general operation and the bursary fund, which may include some form of community event and active participation. ABSW members also respond to individual requests from community members for consultation, advice, and assistance on various social problems.

Looking Forward: The Future of ABSW

As a volunteer group ABSW has had an impact on the community, and their activities and initiatives have helped to combat racism through both personal and institutional change. However, the group is at a crossroads and change is inevitable. The small group of volunteers cannot possibly meet the social welfare needs of the Black community. Through past and current initiatives ABSW has learned that the fight to eradicate racism must involve both perpetrators and survivors. We have learned to work in partnership with the social work community and the grassroots African Nova Scotian community. Perhaps the best way forward is to extend that partnership to include government in our efforts to change child welfare and other social services in order to meet the unique needs of Black citizens in Nova Scotia.

A vision for the future of ABSW is to have permanent and sustainable funding to provide consistency in the support provided to the African Nova Scotian community. All of the initiatives discussed in this article have been supported by volunteerism and/or limited grant funding. Due to such limitations it has been a challenge to keep programs running on a long-term basis. One possibility is forming a network with the newly established government Office of African Nova Scotian Affairs. ABSW hopes to continue to provide support for African Nova Scotian social workers and community members as well as to look at further opportunities for growth and redevelopment.

References

ABSW (1988). Conference on the Family (Unpublished Report).

Barkley, J. (1985). *An examination of the attitudes and knowledge base of non-Black social workers, counsellors and social service workers regarding the Black community in an urban area of Nova Scotia.* Unpublished Master of Social Work Thesis, Dalhousie University. Halifax, Nova Scotia.

Bernard, W.T. (1988). Black families and family therapy in Nova Scotia. In D.E. More & J.H. Morrison (Eds.), *Work, ethnicity and oral history.* Halifax: International Education Centre. p. 81-88.

Bernard, W.T. (1996). *Survival & success: As defined by Black men in Sheffield, England, & Halifax, Canada.* Unpublished Doctoral Thesis. University of Sheffield, Sheffield.

Bernard, W.T., Lucas-White, L., & Moore, D. (1993). Triple jeopardy: assessing life experiences of Black Nova Scotia women from a social work perspective. *Canadian Social Work Review 10*(2), 256-273.

Bernard, W.T., MacDonald, N. & Wien, F. (2005). *The labour market experience of social work graduates: Exploring the role of affirmative action in education.* Toronto: The Canadian Race Relations Foundation.

Bernard, W.T. and Thomas, G. (1991) Social services sensitivity training project report. *Canadian Social Work Review 8*(2), CASSW/ACCESS, Ottawa, Canada.

Bryan, A. (1992). Working with Black single mothers: Myths and reality. In M. Longan & L. Day (Eds.), *Women, oppression and social work: issues in anti-discriminatory practice* (pp. 169-187). London: Routledge.

Iglehart, A. & Becerra, R. (1996). Social work and the ethnic agency: a history of neglect. *Journal of Multicultural Social Work*, 4(1), 1-17.

Johnson, B. (1991). *Black perspectives on foster care: A project exploring the experience of foster care placement on Black children placed in white foster homes.* Unpublished Master of Social Work Research Project, School of Social Work, Dalhousie University.

MacKinnon, F.R. (2004). *Reflections: 55 years in public service in Nova Scotia.* Halifax: Fernwood Publishing.

Marsman, Veronica (1993). *The identity of the bi-racial child.* Unpublished Master of Social Work Thesis, Dalhousie University, Halifax, Nova Scotia.

Turner, S.M. & Jones, R.T. (Eds) (1982). *Behavior modification in Black populations: psychological issues and empirical findings.* New York: Plenum Press.

Section Two:

Making Change Happen:
New Pathways for
Black Social Workers

Chapter 4

Partnering for Connectedness in the Community

Lynda Thomas

I come from a large family and there were twelve brothers and sisters. There was a whole generation older than we were and I have brothers and sisters who are about twenty-two to twenty-five years older than me, literally old enough to be my parents. It was quite a unique situation where I was being parented by older siblings.

My father was born in Dartmouth but my mother was born in Halifax. My mother's name was Ada Maxwell and my father's name was Joseph Tynes. My father worked as an ironworker at the Shipyards at the Dartmouth Marine Slips. He only had a grade three education but he was functionally literate because my mother taught him to read and write. For a woman of my mother's generation, a Black woman of her time, she was quite educated, having a grade nine education. She was born in 1914 and my father in 1911.

My family was a very nurturing one and I grew up in the sixties. I was in elementary school in the sixties and in junior high in the early seventies. My mother was a very giving, nurturing woman who was always in the home because she didn't work outside of it. I have two older sisters who went into the nursing profession. One was a Certified Nursing Assistant and the other was a Registered Nurse.

Education was really pushed as something to strive for in my family and reading was important because my mother encouraged us to read. We grew up in a really tiny house down by the railroad tracks in Dartmouth. It was just a little house full of people and my mother would have us read to her while she was busy doing her housework and you would hear her say, "Speak louder because I can't hear you. You have to speak louder." Or she would say, "Speak more clearly. I can hear you but I don't know what you're saying. Pronounce your words more clearly." Reading was very important and my mother read, my father read, we all read and we were all very proud of having library cards. We were always encouraged to go to the library so that getting an education was just expected and we were expected and encouraged to do the very best we could, and we did our best.

I was raised in the Catholic Church and as a very young girl, I wanted to be a nun and maybe that's where wanting to do some type of helping profession started for me. I had some very good relationships with nuns and I loved spending time at the convent. As I got to be a teenager, I met boys and the idea of becoming a nun fizzled out but I still wanted to go into the helping profession.

My very early memories of being in elementary school are not pleasant. I can remember being in the third grade and we were learning math, but for one reason or another I didn't understand what the teacher was trying to tell us. Looking back, it was so simple, but I can just remember being terrified and not being able to think straight. It felt like she was talking from a distance and I didn't understand what she was telling me. She became very angry with me, and I was the only Black child in that classroom. My family was the only Black family in that school. Then she went to her desk and took out what looked like something we used to

call Graham Wafer biscuits. They were square shaped and chocolate coated. She held it up first and said, "What is this? This is
one whole. Repeat after me." So I did. I said, "It's one whole." She
took her knife and hacked it in half and said, "Now what is this?
Two halves." So I repeated it, and so on and so forth; she cut it in
quarters. Then she asked, "Now do you understand?" Well, I don't
know if I understood or not but I told her yes because I was terrified. Then she went on to say, "Thank you very much for ruining
my recess." So I went out to the playground and all the little white
kids were mad at me because one of the little white girls had given
the teacher the biscuit for recess.

I can remember raising my hand in class and being told, "Put
your hand down. Stop waving your hand around." I also remember being excluded and being called names like "nigger" out on the
playground and I got into a lot of fights. I began to fight at a very
young age and that just seemed to be how I tried to solve things.
I got into trouble many times for fighting. First of all my mother
didn't allow us to fight, so I'd get in trouble at home if I got in
a fight and I'd get in trouble at school. It didn't matter who was
right or who was wrong. The teachers always took sides with the
white children. Even if you said they called you a name, the teachers would ask, "What did they call you?" Well, I wasn't comfortable with saying, "She called me a nigger," especially in the sixties.
Then the teachers would say things like, "Sticks and stones will
break your bones" kind of thing. It all just left a real sour taste in
my mouth for school and I didn't like school.

In my very early years, I was in public school and then I
went to St. Peter's Catholic School later on for junior high. I liked
being there and I liked being with the nuns. I just felt that I was
more accepted there, but as I got older it was just as racist there.
I can remember being in grade seven and there was one nun, a
very elderly woman, and she was reading aloud to us from *The
Adventures of Tom Sawyer* with all the derogatory tones about Black
people and I was just mortified and didn't know what to do. So
I went home and I didn't tell my mother because my mother and
father were from the very old school. I couldn't see them going

forward and doing anything about it. I went to one of my older siblings, my sister Maxine, who wasn't that much older than me, and told her. She wrote a note to the nun and it talked about how wrong it was to read this and how it left me feeling. I never heard anymore about it but she stopped reading.

I think I started to understand about racism when there began to be a separation. It was as if a line was drawn in the sand between me and other white middle-class girls who were my peers. All of a sudden, people were pairing off and doing things and I was less included, more and more excluded. I can remember going to a girl's house one evening. There was a group of us girls and we went to call on her because we were all going somewhere together. We were young and in junior high. The girl came to the door and said to me, "Lynda, can you wait outside? Because you're not allowed to come in." All the other girls were allowed to go in. I can remember going to a party at another girl's house and knocking on the door and there were lots of people in the house, her family and her friends, and some man hollered out, "If you're white come in. If you're a nigger stay out." What do you do? You're fourteen or fifteen, what do you do? Being fourteen or fifteen back then was a lot less sophisticated and we were less aware of issues then than children are today.

I left school in grade ten. I was told I had to go back to school, but before I could go back I found out that I was pregnant. Then I stayed home. I don't ever recall seeing any girls my age who were pregnant in those days. A couple of years after me, I saw it happening, but not at my time. There were no girls in high school who were pregnant because they discouraged you from going to school when you became pregnant.

I started trying to go back to school when my baby was about six or seven months old because it was a given that you had to get an education. I tried to go to Dartmouth High, but I just couldn't do it. I couldn't settle into it so I went to night school. I got my grade ten through night school and about a year later, I wrote my GED and got my grade twelve.

I got married on my daughter's third birthday. We got married, and my family was always very supportive of my husband and me and they encouraged him to continue schooling. At that time, he was in vocational school and doing a plumbing trade. My dad died suddenly; he passed away when my baby was nine months old.

It was quite a struggle and I stayed home with the kids and seldom worked. When I worked, it had to be jobs where I could take my kids. Once I got a job in the school as a teacher's aide for a while and so I could be in school with the kids when they were there. Then when they got a little older, I decided I had to build a career for myself. My mother always encouraged that. She'd say, "You can't depend on anyone but the Lord above and that almighty buck. Depend on yourself, get your own, have your own, and be able to stand on your own." She really encouraged me to continue. She'd also say, "Make a living for yourself."

I knew I always wanted to work with people and I always used to think I'd like to work with youths and I heard about a course they were offering at Community College at the Nova Scotia Institute of Technology, the Community Service Workers Course. That was back in the eighties and I applied for it and I got in. I really liked it, I really enjoyed the course. Then after that, during that year I applied to the School of Social Work. I was really frightened; I thought that I couldn't do it. I just didn't have the confidence. I didn't see myself going to university. Although I have a sister who had gone through university, I just didn't see that it was modeled for me. I never had a Black teacher; I just didn't see a whole lot of that. I still saw myself as a dropout but I applied and I was really surprised when I got in and I was really afraid to go.

My sister Pat, who was a year younger than I, went on the bus to Halifax with me during the summer. It was a kind of rehearsal to prepare me because I was afraid that I would not be able to find my way around. We would go around, walk around the campus and get acquainted with it. My mom kept telling me, "Oh, you can do it." At this point, I was married with two children.

They allowed me to go directly into the BSW program and then I could take a few electives that I needed at the main body of the university, with some prerequisites, which I could work off at the same time as my degree. That was in 1986.

I was a little overwhelmed. But it was like most situations that were new. I was always hoping to see someone who I could identify with, someone who reflected my race or culture; I never saw them of course. For the first couple of years in the program there were no other Black students in my classes. Some of the professors there were very nice and friendly and attempted to be helpful, but somehow I found it really condescending and it just reminded me of the teachers I had who thought they were being good to me, but really they were just undermining my abilities or minimizing my potential by talking to me in condescending manners and thinking I didn't understand things. I always had that sense during that first year, especially from certain professors who meant well. I graduated in 1990.

In class discussions, I was expected to be an expert on Black issues. Sometimes I was singled out and asked, "Can you speak to that, Lynda? Do you have any comments for the group on that?" Or they'd ask, "What was your experience or what would be politically correct?" It made me very uncomfortable and I would say I can only speak in terms of my own experience and I am not the Black experience. I was somehow expected to be able to speak for the Black race and I was uncomfortable doing that, knowing that other people were hanging on to every word and that whatever I said would be taken as gospel and then the Black experience as a whole would be misinterpreted or worse. During my last year there were a few other Black students.

I learned a great deal from my field placement and I'm really pleased that I was able to do it where I did, within the Halifax North community. It really put me in touch with the issues that were affecting my own people and I was able to be a part of building some initiatives that could help others. I was also learning how to help mobilize people; I think that's what it taught me the most. Also, I was really pleased to be there because of Joan Mendez, who was my agency field instructor. She was so supportive and I didn't have to explain things to her. She just knew because she was a

Black woman and I didn't have to say I'm really scared because my faculty field advisor is racist. I could say that to her and she knew. I didn't have to prove it, she knew. I could tell her about things that happened and things that were said and she knew it and she was able to advocate on my behalf and that was really helpful because I almost quit. I was just literally in tears, and I'm not of that nature. I am not one to give up and crumble, but it was like I was up against it and it wasn't worth it to me. It wasn't worth my peace of mind.

My strongest memory of my years at the School of Social Work is the day that I felt that I could not continue. At the time, I was feeling overwhelmed and quite lost in an environment where I didn't belong, where I couldn't relate and where I was not reflected in the faces or attitudes of the faculty or students.

Entering the Maritime[1] School of Social Work, as a mature student and mother of two young children, I was excited and looked forward to beginning studies that would allow me to fulfill my long-time goal of becoming a social worker. I had expected to be met with challenges but was determined to work hard and to be successful. Having dropped out of the education system at a young age because of the racist and stereotypical attitudes of educators, to find myself at the School of Social Work facing these same attitudes and issues left me feeling disillusioned, to say the least. The general atmosphere at the school left me feeling isolated and stressed.

I felt that my faculty field advisor talked to me in a way that was very disrespectful. I found that she didn't value my experience, didn't even respect the fact that I had the ability to lay out my own learning objectives. She questioned every thing that I did, and I don't mean in a manner that was professionally critical or enabling. It was just really hard-nosed and she also used derogatory terms when talking about the community. She said things like "Those people," and "You people" or "Your people," and it just got to be very stressful. It was stressful because she was in a position

---

1. The name Maritime School of Social Work was changed to Dalhousie School of Social Work (DSSW) in 2004. Many of the contributors in the book are graduates or current students of the DSSW.

where she could make or break me, and I didn't know how far I could go in defending myself to her or where to go with it. It got to the point where I just thought, this isn't going to work; I may as well just throw it in because I'm not even going to be able to pass my field placement.

After one particularly difficult conversation with my faculty field advisor which left me feeling berated and defeated, I disclosed my feelings to my agency field instructor, a feisty African Nova Scotian woman who was the director of a community agency that provided programs and support for single parent women in the North End Halifax community. She was a veteran community worker and a person who does not mince words; I know that she talked to my faculty field instructor. I know she had quite the conversation with her. I don't know what she did after that but all I know is in my mailbox at school there was a notification that I was now to have a new faculty field instructor and it would be Dr. Wanda Thomas Bernard. I didn't even know her. All I knew was that she was a Black woman and I was so happy. I just thought, "Oh thank you, Lord!"

I did not mind if I had to battle to get through, and if I was not making the grade and there were things I had to work on or if I had to take an incomplete or whatever – I'll know it was not because my skin is black. It was really, truly all about learning for me and I didn't mind being told that I had to do better. Previously, I couldn't figure out if it was me or the white faculty marking us with the same brush. For instance, I felt that I had adequate writing skills and that writing was one of my strong points, but it got to a point when I started doubting my ability. I had confided this to one professor who said to me, "Don't ever let anyone tell you that you don't have good writing skills because you do, and there's far too much of that happening here." That just sent me a mixed message and I was thinking, "It's easy for you to say that because you have the power, but I have no power in this situation."

I was at the end of my first degree when I had my first Black teacher in my life! In all of my educational life I had never ever had a Black educator until I had Wanda Thomas Bernard. The experience in itself brought to me an immediate sense of relief and more importantly, hope. After meeting with her, I felt validated and supported for the first time while at the School of Social Work.

I was able to continue my studies and successfully complete the BSW program. Upon reflection of my years at the School of Social Work and the years that I have spent working in the community, I realize that it is due to the support of other African Nova Scotian social workers that I get through. It is my involvement with committees such as ABSW that enable me to deal with the stresses of systemic racism that I encounter in my work in this field.

In my job, we provide employment services to the community. It's very clear what those services should be in terms of back to work action plans to get people ready for employment. My degree really is helpful because it helps with the administration of people here in the community by guiding my team into providing quality service to people, treating people with the utmost respect and dignity. It also equips me to be empathetic toward people and to look at the barriers to employment and to counsel around those barriers more effectively and be supportive in helping people fill the gaps and fill their needs. It is those barriers to employment that are the roadblocks for people. Barriers could be anything from homelessness to addictions, to poor health or literacy issues. There could be any number of issues and my social work background really helps me to administer to the community. Also, it helps me to appreciate the fact that this is in our community and that the community should be well served by this service, by this project. I think that my social work background has really helped me a great deal to deliver this program.

I think that educators have to be sensitive and aware of cultural differences, because they do exist, and those differences affect us in a lot of ways in what we have to offer and how we can do business together. It affects how we learn together, how we learn from each other, in that people of different cultural backgrounds have different experiences, and they have a different way of talking and communicating within their various cultures. It isn't always the Eurocentric way. Even in my work here, we have people from all different socioeconomic and cultural backgrounds who come in here and I think cultural sensitivity and awareness goes a very long way in understanding the needs of people. This means their educational needs, if you're an educator, or their employment needs if you are working in my type of work environment, providing employment services. There's a connectedness in the community because we all have to partner. I think the educational institutions have to partner with the community and I think that's how these things can be built upon, and educators, in terms of how to be all-inclusive, can acquire the skills.

I have worked with a lot of social workers, both Black and white, over the years but my connection and involvement in ABSW has been really good for me. It really keeps me in touch, because sometimes I feel like I'm sort of floating away from the world of social work because there are all sorts of connections to social work agencies and I work in the community. ABSW keeps me connected, which is really good.

Chapter 5

Something Good Out of North Preston

Anne Simmons

I still live in the community of North Preston where I grew up. My experience growing up in the community is a positive one and I see it as an asset. North Preston is a community where everybody looked out for everybody. I don't mean looking just to make sure they were safe. It was a community where several families provided food, clothing and other such items for any child, and it was not necessarily out of a sense of need but out of a sense of just general sharing and communality. Ours was a community which helped and always extended a hand, regardless of who you were or what family you came from. One of the things which stands out most in my mind is the communal response to bereavement. My mom died when I was eight. She was a schoolteacher in the school at North Preston. She was diagnosed with cancer and with nine children, that was a cause of great stress. Many people wondered how our father would cope with looking after the children. I remember that everybody helped.

My mom's death was very difficult for me, coming at such a young age. She died when she was in her thirties and I think my dad was also in his thirties or late twenties. Prior to her death, she had given birth to my younger brother. I recall Mom being pregnant and I also recall her going for treatment. Even though we were young, my mom was able to tell us that she was sick. We didn't know it was cancer. My dad, who was not much of a talker, never talked about it. He was a good provider. He made sure that there was food and clothing. He was also very mindful of the overall safety of the family. My mom was the talker. She was the person who would say, "You know, I'm sick." I remember her telling my older sister, my brother and I that she was okay and saying, "Mommy's going to be okay but I want you to be educated. I want you to love everybody. I want you to know the Lord." I used to wonder, "Why is Mom telling us all this?" Now that I am older it all comes back to me.

I'm the third oldest of nine children. Our paternal grandmother and great-grandmother as well as our aunts and uncles from North Preston were really remarkable. Mother's mother came from Mulgrave and we have family from Tracadie and Sunnyville. We never went without and if I try and imagine a situation today where there are nine children with a father out of the home and a mother diagnosed with cancer, given the complications of long-term care, I am sure that the child welfare system would have to be involved at some point, if only to ensure that a proper plan was in place to care for the children. My mom and my dad and the family in North Preston gave me the foundation for helping. It was a kind of helping that was genuine, helping from the heart, and it is my honest belief that's why I became a social worker, working with family. It is because of that and my belief in God that I became the person I am today.

Reminiscing on my life growing up in North Preston and the death of my mother, it is my honest belief that we were destined to be a part of the community of North Preston. I believe that it was not by chance: it was designed that way by God so that although my mother's travels in life were short, during that brief period on earth she taught school, she became a friend to everybody in the community and my dad talked about how nice she was.

When dad remarried, he was happy and my stepmom is still living today. Through that process he became the deacon in the church and she's now a pastor. Being a parent and given my large family, I became actively involved in the community, as a volunteer teaching Sunday school. I've been teaching since I was sixteen. I also sing in the choir, and when someone dies I take the family some food, and if someone is getting married I help out. It all comes from a sense of community but it's not as tight as it used to be.

The thing about coming from the community, which I find demoralizing, is the fact that a lot of people look down on North Preston. We hear people saying, "Nothing good comes out of North Preston." Unfortunately, there are those who readily buy into that stereotype and so they fail to make something of themselves. I believe I took my upbringing and looked at it and decided that something good would come out of North Preston. Being the first social worker who graduated from the community, I looked at it as a challenge to give someone else an experience or to be a role model to somebody so there would many more firsts. I believed there would also be many other people who would want to do this work. There would be people, young men and young women, who would want to work with family and keep the close-knit community and work within the community.

It was hard, it was very hard. I never talked to anybody about it until I got to the Maritime School of Social Work. Dr. Wanda Thomas Bernard was my professor and I only talked about it where I felt it was okay to talk about it and because I knew she would understand, coming from a Black community herself. The stigma was really hard to deal with. In the university people would ask questions, "Oh, where are you from?" I would say North Preston but they would say, "No, you can't be from North Preston. Maybe you are living there or maybe you found a home there," but I would insist that I was born and raised in North Preston. It was when they questioned me that I realized that "Oh my God, these people thought that nobody graduating or studying in the university could come from North Preston." That was a weight that I carried for a while.

In elementary school, I always wanted to learn. My mom was a schoolteacher so education, homework, had to be done and you had to do it right and do it properly. I grew up with the idea that homework came first. We also had to be up on the current news and how it affected us and our community or how it might affect it in the future. Being the daughter of a schoolteacher, of course I was always expected to be smart.

I went to W. Evans and Nelson Whynder Elementary Schools. Both were segregated schools and it was not a challenge. When I got into junior high I was also at the top of the class and did advanced courses and sciences. I was supposed to go to Graham Creighton for my junior high but it was overcrowded so I went to Humber Park. They made it a junior high when I was in grade seven. It was not a completely segregated school. The primary grades to grade six were segregated; it was all Black in the community of Cherry Brook. I left Humber Park and went to Sir Robert Borden. I finished my grade seven and then grade eight at Sir Robert Borden.

Grades nine, ten, eleven, and twelve were at Graham Creighton. In grade eleven, we had a lot of Black students. I remember going into the office of the guidance counsellor and saying, "I'm going to university." All the teachers and my reports said I was an excellent student. I took all academic courses. My dad and my stepmom would go to parent-teacher meetings and were told, "Anne's doing fine, no problem."

I went to the guidance counsellor because I always wanted to go to university. He asked, "Where do you live?" He got the file out and he said, "Well, Ms. Simmonds, you're getting the Negro Fund." Back then we used to get some financial assistance twice a year and they used to call it the Negro Fund. At Easter and Christmas the Department of Education would give fifty dollars to everybody who was what they called "Negro." All the Black kids would be called to come down to the office and we'd get our cheque. It was my understanding that the guidance counsellor had to identify who all the Black students were at that time.

When I went to him and said, "I want to go to university," he went to my file and said, "Oh yeah, you will receive the Negro Fund. Well, you know you're getting the Negro Fund but they are not going to let you in the university." I was alarmed and thought, "Oh, my God! Anne, what are you going to do?" I thought about it and I decided this was not a battle for my dad, this was my battle.

I went to Mr. Brad Barton, an African Nova Scotian who was the principal at the time. I said, "Mr. Barton, I want to go to university," and Mr. Barton said, "Anne, there's no problem." I explained what the guidance counsellor had said, and asked him to find out what he meant. Mr. Barton intervened and I did go to university, but I honestly believe the guidance counsellor didn't want me to.

I was inspired to go to university because I knew that in order for me to do what I needed to do, I needed to believe in myself. Even though there were barriers put up by the guidance counsellor, when I come across obstacles like that, I rise above the occasion. I rise above such statements; I rise above what others think of me. Coming from the community of North Preston, I learned to rise above these types of issues. Everything there that was negative, I tried to turn positive for myself. I always wanted to go higher.

I don't want to plateau in anything I do and education is something that I just didn't want to end in grade twelve, even though back then in the seventies, grade twelve was like a university degree to get through because it was very difficult. The statistics for Black people graduating were not that great. I believed in myself and I knew I could do the work. Nobody talked me into it. I remember saying to my dad, "I want to go to university" and he responded, "Well Anne, I will be here for you." Financially it was difficult because there were nine of us. I had to live on campus because we didn't have any form of public transportation at that time.

I did my first degree at Saint Mary's University, and I remember one professor talking about deviance. He was talking about some of the communities in the United States and he made a reference about similarities to the Black community here in Halifax and North Preston. My heart stopped because I was from North Preston. He drew a similarity to people being killed and raped and the deviants of society.

I was insulted, and I thought, "Oh my God, here's a class of a hundred people and here is this professor talking about a community that he really doesn't know anything about." Some of my classmates knew I was from North Preston because we had become friends. It was as if my heart stopped and I thought to myself, "Anne, what do you do? If you put your hand up, he's going to say, well, this is what the literature says." I remember also thinking, "Anne, you can't finish this course without letting him know that you are from the community and the mistake that he made and how he hurt you."

It went on for two months and I prayed about it, but eventually I went to the professor and I told him what he said in the class on deviance and the unfair comparison he made. I told him I was from North Preston. He said, "Ms. Simmonds, you might know somebody from there." I explained that I was actually from the community of North Preston but that I was living on campus.

Then he said, "Oh, Ms. Simmonds, why didn't you tell me? You could have taught the class!" I said, "Sir, I am offended by that comment. Teach the class on deviance? What are you talking about? You got up and you made an inaccurate comparison of my home to a community in the United States. There's no mugging, there's no killing, there's no drive-by shootings in my community." This was in the seventies and there was none of that.

I said, "You made references to statistics; you need to show me those statistics." Then he admitted, "I don't have any." So I insisted, "Then you need to go back and correct your class." My heart was pounding because I thought he was going to fail me if I challenged him. I was about eighteen and everybody said he had been teaching for so long. People had warned me, "Don't challenge him, wait until you get your grade." But I said, "I can't wait. This man put down my community, where my father and my mother, the community is so positive. He's putting it down and I can't have members of my class believing him."

He corrected himself. He went back and I remember he made this comment: "I stand to be corrected. There's a young lady in the class who is from the community and I certainly was wrong." I was the only Black person in the class and of course everybody knew it was me. That day, a lot of people came up and thanked me for standing up.

The transition to university was a challenge, but I fondly recall joining with the other Black students at Saint Mary's and forming an association. We supported each other, and we helped the communities. We did tutoring programs in all of the local Black communities and also helped mentor the junior and senior high school students about higher education. We got to know everybody so well because the message that we wanted to put out was that "You can be anybody. You too can come to the university. Don't let anybody kill your dream." And it worked.

I finished my first degree in 1977 and went on to work. I worked at Community Care, as a social work aide, placing the old, sick or disabled into nursing homes. I didn't like that because I came from a community which didn't put loved ones into nursing homes, but I did it for eight months. Following my job at Community Services, I wanted to work with children. Having a Bachelor of Arts degree, everything that I applied for back then, I was told I was too qualified. So I started work at a day care centre and enjoyed that because I could do programming with the children and it also allowed me to work with parents. It was while I was there that I realized that I needed to go back to school again because I had reached a plateau in my employment.

I decided I wanted to go to the Maritime School of Social Work. That was back in the late seventies or early eighties. Then I became pregnant with my daughter; it was in 1992 and I still worked as a single parent. I needed a job that was going to allow me to work during the day and go to school at night because I needed to provide for my daughter. Then a job vacancy came in the newspaper for a Case Aide to provide transport and to supervise parent-child visits and assist with a social worker with the Children's Aid Society (CAS) of Halifax.

I got the job, and during the first year I went to team meetings and told them about the community. Social workers at that time were struggling with how to interact with the Black communities. I felt we needed to get to know the community; we needed to ask the person, "Who are the people in your community? Who are the supports in your community?" We needed to tell them, "I want to know about your community. How were you brought up?" It was not enough to simply read the case study, and then try to apply the same case plan to everybody. Not everybody did what people assumed they were doing. Some people valued my input and I remember my supervisor saying, "You can't be a Case Aide all your life. You're too valuable; you're an asset." I also remember my supervisor, the agency director, Marilyn Peers, and Wanda Thomas Bernard saying, "You need to go into social work."

Wanda Thomas Bernard from the Association of Black Social Workers (ABSW) would come in to the CAS and do workshops with our staff about culture and looking at our employers, she would advise that we needed to hire more Black workers. The agency worked very closely with her and really took her suggestions even on the issue of same race adoption.

I eventually went to the Maritime School of Social Work, and I found that it was another world. I said, "Lord, you are not going to give me anything I cannot bear." I couldn't believe some of the stuff that they were reading in case studies. In addition, meeting people from other communities, I was amazed that they didn't have the grassroots orientation that I had. Coming from my community gave me so much, because of the sense of community, and it was important to becoming a social worker since a lot of it was about how people grow up, how people become part of their community and how to make the system work. Some of the classes involved standing out and speaking out about who you were and standing up and saying that's not what it's like. We had some students who were very green, because their upbringing wasn't like that. They said, "Well, I wouldn't go beyond the Macdonald Bridge." You had to really check them, because you couldn't have people saying that about your community.

I wanted to go through the educational process so that I could get stronger and go to the next process in the field. I put my life experiences into all of my papers. All the professors would say, "You should have expanded more on that." In 1987, when the school was being accredited, I was asked to be interviewed. The accreditation team asked, "If there's one thing that you could change, what would it be?" I talked about how we needed a course, not a half time, not an elective, but a mandatory course where we would talk about culture, particularly Black culture. I felt this was necessary because we were graduating students who were getting out into the community and making comments that were racist. I felt that the School needed to take the initiative. When Wanda Thomas Bernard was hired it was just like the sun had finally come out or a brighter light came on. She challenged me. It was like a confirmation that everything I put up with – from junior high, to my mother's death and the demoralizing comments about my community – had all been worth the trouble because here was a confirmation that things were going to be okay.

Just before we graduated, Wanda Thomas Bernard came in to our class and spoke about the importance of standing up, as a Black person, and that identity is about who we are and believing in ourselves. I lived that. I wove all my experiences into my practice. I remember when I was doing my Field II, I wanted to look at the cultural perspective and how we needed to weave it into our practice at the agency. Out of my proposal about looking at the cultural perspective of placing children into Black homes and getting more Black foster homes and out of that field practice, the CAS created a Placement Worker and hired a social worker to do recruitment of Black foster and adopted homes.

The other thing that was happening back then was that the workers didn't know where to put children who were of mixed race. A colleague and I ran a cultural group one Saturday with children of mixed race. We asked, "When you look in the mirror, who do you see? Who do you identify yourself with?" A lot of them did not know how to say the word Black. But it was okay, because we got literature and we put supports in place for them.

Being a child protection worker and living in an open community like North Preston is very challenging. You can't go home and erase your work, but I try to get people to separate me from my work and to see me in different roles. There are times when you get a comment either from within the agency or within the system itself, even right up to the legal system when talking about children. A child is not just a name on paper. It's somebody's child and you have to educate them on that too. It's not about winning or losing; it's about talking – about families, about putting them back together, putting them back into the community and ensuring that there's a community for them to go back to. There are nights when I had to stay up through the night because I'm doing case planning in my head because the system didn't fit the case of a particular Black child. I ask myself, "How do you make it fit, Anne?" I have lost a lot of sleep.

I do not give in to stress because I know that on Sunday, I would go back to Sunday school and be reminded of my blessings. I think I came to the point where I realized that I was so blessed that I couldn't become stressed because I needed to move and do something creative or had to make the case plan fit so this child could make it in their home and in their community. I still have struggles today. We work in a system where there isn't a lot of money. That speaks to the integrity of the family, but it's up to me to put it together so that it can fit – that's a struggle because every case is different and it really depends on what you have to work with.

I believe that until those who are in policy-making positions make a conscious effort to start meeting the community that we work in, they cannot make policies that are going to fit our clients. I see my race as a factor in determining the opportunities available. I think they acknowledge who I am and how resourceful and professional I am. Several times when I call clients who are not Black for the first time and I say I'm Ms. Simmonds, and then I get to the door, they don't want to open the door. When they open it, I deal with it right away. I say, "You probably assumed that I was a Caucasian woman. No, I am not. I am here, I will be very professional with you and I just want to know that you're feeling comfortable." If they say, "I don't want a Black worker," I will take it back to my supervisor and say, "I don't want to be a struggle in anybody's life" and I hope that my colleagues are aware of that when Black clients say, "I don't want a white worker."

I've gone through experiences where I've been called a "nigger" in court. I stopped my testimony and addressed the court to deal with it. I've been called a nigger when working with several families and I've asked the agency to address it. They had their agency lawyer address it. I have no tolerance with that. Struggles are one thing; for me, it is important how I deal with it. You can name it, claim it, and move on.

I find almost on a weekly basis, because of the system we work in which moves so fast, that your ears and your eyes have to be open all the time because the minute you allow something to slip, it becomes the norm, and I know that my colleagues respect my correction. They'll come back with an apology. I'm aware that they weren't brought up the same way I was and I'm nice about it. I always tell them if it was somebody else that you approached in the community or a client they may not be as sensitive as I am, or they may be very sensitive to it. My colleagues call on me when they are going out to deal with clients who are not white. I have had colleagues coming back, saying my best clients were so and so, because they got to tell their story.

I always tell my colleagues, have that person tell their story. Don't put everybody in a stereotypical box based on what you grew up believing or your assumption about them. Let them tell their story, and if there is something positive, you pull from it and build on it. Some of them do. I recently had a colleague who turned her chair around and hugged me and said, "I value everything you're telling me."

I thank God for one of my colleagues, who has been there for years. She worked in the Black community for years, and she knows about the Black family, the importance of it, and how it takes a Black community to raise a Black child. She incorporates that in her practice. The interesting thing is that she was incorporating that into her practice before I became a social worker. Those are the kinds of things that make me want to go back to work on Monday mornings.

I regret that I haven't been active in the Association of Black Social Workers because of family obligations. But now that the children are older I see myself becoming more active in the Association. It's nice to know that the organization is there for us to talk about things. It also gives us the opportunity as Black social workers to do projects or to put in place different programs that are going to benefit the greater community. I've always talked about the Black United Front. I just hope someone will make government accountable in terms of giving funding to ABSW so that we can do work. I honestly believe that having ABSW tied into agencies, and not only Child Protection but also Income Assistance and Housing, will give better service to our Black clients or people who need to take up a service.

We have professional social workers who know the system; they can make the system work effectively and more quickly for the clients. That's not there now, and I hope that one day someone will recognize that. I don't know if the Minister of African Nova Scotian Affairs will pay attention because that was money that was supposed to be given back to the Black community to look at the social issues of Black people. Who better to give it to when you have a group of professionals such as social workers who have gone through the school? I believe that the Association of Black Social Workers can do it, because I know on an individual basis, I have done it. I have known other colleagues that are in the Association who have done it.

I think that there would be more strength in that we can get more service for our clients, for our children, for our elders and for our sick if somebody was there to fill in the gap, and I think ABSW can do it. We have the education, we have the experience, we advocate for our clients in the child welfare system, which is connected to all those other issues – housing, day care, the elderly, and mental health. I think that there would be less money to be spent in the legal system because fewer cases would have to go to court. I know that there would be better service to the clients. And also, it would be a form of protection, in the sense of keeping the community a community because we are in the community, we are in the homes.

From my own experience, I think we need to believe in ourselves. Always set higher goals for yourself. I have always said we need to challenge the person who says, "Because you're from North Preston, you're not going to be nobody." I don't know who even said it, but I tell myself, never say that, always say something good will always come out of North Preston. Always turn a negative phase or phrase into a positive. Look at the barriers as a form of learning and rise above them, and if you can't do it alone, there are people who can help you. If you fill in the gap for somebody, it is my spiritual belief that what you give, you will get back tenfold. I've seen that, I know that, I have experienced it. And when you give, don't expect anything in return; give with a free heart and that's not just financially or materially, even just giving advice, a kind word to somebody, it will come back tenfold. It's not just about physical giving, it is also about words.

Whenever I come across people who say, "I want to become a social worker," my first thought is this: believe in yourself, be spiritually grounded and always do and say to people only what you want them to say and do to you. You want good for yourself; want good for somebody else. You want no harm to come to you; don't bring harm to somebody else. You want your family to stay together; work to have other people's family stay together. Take a seed; sow a seed — we all should look on ourselves as part of a garden.

Anything that you want in life that's going to be successful is not going to be easy. You don't want a degree because you are a "token Black." You don't want to be a social worker if they have to hire you only because you are Black. You want them to take into consideration the fact that you have something to offer, your credibility and your accountability. Believe in yourself – tell yourself, "I can do this job. I can move mountains to make a difference."

I honestly believe I have moved mountains in my professional work. I've taken risks which others have benefited from. Take risks even when you feel that you're alone. People may not come up and say that you are doing a good job immediately, but at the end of it, they will tell you. And when they tell you, say, "Okay, that project is done, where do I go next? What do I change next?"

The world of child welfare, child protection, is always growing, always changing and it's a tailspin and I always see myself in the bottom or in the top of the tailspin. I say to myself, "Anne, if you are going to spin off, where do you want to be next? How can you help someone next?"

Chapter 6

Following in Secret Steps

Satie Borden

From the ages of seven to twenty-one, I was in the care and custody of Shelburne Children's Aid Society. I was placed in the permanent care and custody of a child protection agency because of my biological mother's mental health and substance abuse problem.

My first and second foster care placements were with non-African Nova Scotia families. The two families were white. Adult relatives of my biological mother were approached about providing a foster home placement for me; however, their response was no because they were worried that there would be interference from my mother.

The first foster home placement was with the child care provider and her family members; my biological mother arranged this for me when she was a full-time employee at the hospital in the community where we resided. The duration of the first foster home placement was less than a year because of the problems that transpired between the biological children of the foster parents and me. The foster parents' biological children made comments, when their parents were not present, that I was not part of their family because I did not physically resemble them. These comments precipitated physical altercations between them and me. Due to the ongoing rivalry and the foster parents' feeling they were unable to deal with this matter as a family, they requested that another placement be arranged.

The second foster home placement was in a community where I was the only African Nova Scotian. Problems in relation to this foster home placement commenced immediately. The first day of school was an event in my life that will never be forgotten. When I entered the school bus, there were two children sitting in the front of the bus who yelled, "Look at the nigger." I remember walking to the back of the bus and crying, while the other students and the bus driver ignored me. Imagine the feelings that a child at the age of seven would experience at this time in his/her life when encountering a situation of this nature and having no support system.

Unfortunately, this was not the end of a first day of school nightmare. Instead of being placed in the proper grade, school personnel placed me in a grade below where I was previously enrolled. It was not until approximately a week later that I was placed in the proper grade. Although being enrolled in the proper class was a positive experience, the racist attitudes of the students prevailed. On a daily basis the white students referred to me using the following terms: "nigger, coon, monkey and blackie." Everyday I would return to the foster home crying. The foster mother tried her hardest to validate my feelings, but it was obvious she did not have the cultural understanding to effectively respond to the racism. I remember she would respond to my emotional state by holding me in her arms and conveying that everything would get better. When I ceased crying she would provide me with one of my favourite treats (for example, cookies or cake) as a means to comfort me.

My memories of the foster mother at the second placement have always remained positive. There was never a day when she did not exhibit the same level of affection toward me as she did with her own children. The foster mother requested early in the placement that I refer to her as "Mom." For a child in care, having a family is very important; therefore, I was ecstatic about being able to refer to her as my mother. My relationship with two of the foster parents' biological children was also positive.

One of the foster parents' children did not appreciate the relationship that I developed with his mother. He responded by referring to me as the "nigger kid, who does not have a family." As a young child it was obvious that he did not want me to be a part of his family. There was one evening when he took me into the woods behind the foster home and tied me to a tree. Prior to departing from the woods, he stated, "You're nothing but a nigger and you're not part of our family, so don't call our parents Mom and Dad because you don't look like us." I remained tied to the tree for what I considered to be a long duration. The temperature outside was cold and it was dark. I remember crying and screaming, but nobody responded and the foster parents' child did not return to release me from the tree. I am unable to recall the specific details, but somehow I managed to loosen the rope used to tie me to the tree.

When I returned to the foster home, the foster parents appeared to be worried about me and communicated that they had been searching for me. The foster parents' child who tied me to the tree was present when I returned home, and did not advise his parents about his physical and emotionally abusive behaviour that resulted in my whereabouts being unknown. The same evening I disclosed to the foster mother the situation that occurred between her son and me. I am unaware of how the foster parents disciplined their son, but approximately a week later I was removed from the foster home.

When I was in my late twenties, the foster child who was physically and emotionally abusive toward me in the second foster home placement approached me in the community. He actually apologized to me for how he treated me when I lived with his family. He then proceeded to introduce me to his partner, who was African Nova Scotian. I have to admit that I was shocked about the race of his partner, considering how racist he was as a child;

however, it must have taken a lot of courage for him to apologize to me.

The contact with my previous foster sibling resulted in me wanting to gain more knowledge about my life during the first two foster care placements. This information was obtained by contacting my social worker and scheduling an appointment to peruse the relevant documents in my "children in care" file. After reading this file, I engaged in a conversation with my social worker about my foster placements with the white families. I was apprised that the second foster parents tried everything to enhance their cultural competence in order for me to remain in their care; however, they had to make the decision that a family of African descent may be able to meet my emotional, physical and social needs better than themselves. Furthermore, as an African Nova Scotian child, I was extremely confused about my identity.

After I was removed from the second foster home placement, my social worker, who was an African Nova Scotian female, continued to pursue locating a culturally appropriate foster home placement for me. Through her persistence, she arranged for me to be placed with my maternal aunt, her partner and their six biological children. The placement adjustment was difficult for me because I was not cognizant of the reasons I was unable to live with my biological mother, who resided within close proximity to my maternal aunt and her family. My biological half sibling resided next door to me, with my maternal grandmother, and was not a foster child. I was placed in three foster homes within less than two years and I questioned if this was a result of my personality. The preceding factors had a negative impact on my emotional state as a young child. I was a nervous child, with low self-esteem, who also exhibited attention-seeking behaviours in an attempt to gain acceptance and love from others.

I remained in the care of my maternal aunt and her family until the age of eighteen, when I graduated high school and was accepted in a university outside my community. There was a period during my adolescence when I was placed outside the care of my maternal aunt and family for approximately a week. I was sent to a group home outside my community. Nobody ever explained to me the justification for the placement change; however, to this day I attribute the situation to my maternal aunt and her partner requesting a respite placement for me. My adolescence also consisted of exhibiting attention-seeking behaviour, coupled with non-compliance with the regulations my maternal aunt and uncle implemented for me, as a means to be accepted by others, especially my peers. Due to the difficulties I encountered adjusting at the group home, and after I made several emotional phone calls to my social worker, arrangements were made for the respite placement to end early and I returned to the care of my maternal aunt and her family.

The experience of having been a child in care and having an African Nova Scotian social worker, who I perceived as a role model, was a positive factor in my life. Unfortunately, a lot of African Nova Scotian children in care are assigned white social workers. This is a result of the child protection agencies in Nova Scotia primarily being staffed with non-African Nova Scotian social workers. For example, in the year of 2005, there were less than ten African Nova Scotian social workers employed in the field of child protection in Nova Scotia. My social worker will always be someone who I will continue to role model myself after, and I have secretly followed in her footsteps. In my opinion, she always advocated for what she believed was in my best interest. One of my goals in life, to be a social worker, was because of her and the influence that she had on my life.

My maternal aunt and some of her biological children also have to be credited for the personal goals that I achieved in life, especially academically. As an adolescent in the care of my maternal family members, there was definitely a fear associated with being disciplined if you did not do well academically. Failing a test or not receiving a high grade average on a test, exam or paper would result in a repercussion of two weeks grounding at the minimum. Grounding within this family consisted of isolation immediately after school and during the weekends, followed by a long list of household chores that took hours per day to complete. Having been raised in a strict household has been a contributing factor today in my life in relation to always setting extremely high standards for myself and others close to my life.

Community life for an African Nova Scotian in a predominately white community consisted of daily experiences of racism. I encountered racism in the public school system and from other students in the community. There were occasions when the children in the community referred to me and other African Nova Scotian children using racist slurs. As a child, I responded to the racism from the other children in a physically aggressive manner. These actions are not something that I am proud of today; however, this was the only mechanism I knew to deal with racism displayed by others within a similar age range.

The racism encountered by members of the school system was blatant my first week of grade eight. My marks in the grade eight academic stream were above the class average, with the exception of French; however, in grade nine I was placed in general classes. Within a short period, my maternal aunt, with the assistance of one of her children, realized that school personnel had enrolled me in general courses. The next day, my aunt and cousin attended the school and the following day I was enrolled in grade nine academic courses with the exception of French.

During my final year of high school I applied to university and to a hairdressing program and was accepted at both. I remember being excited about the opportunity to accompany some of my closest peers to a community-based academic program instead of attending university, which at that time in my life meant many more years of studying. It was not long before my maternal aunt advised that she did not support my enrolment in a hairdressing program; therefore, the only option that I had was to attend university. As the wise old tale indicates, "Listen to the adults in your life because they are usually right." This being said, I left the small community where I lived the majority of my life and went to university approximately a three-hour drive away from my family members.

Although I was raised the majority of my life with family members who were African Nova Scotian, there were aspects of my culture and heritage to which I was oblivious. My African Nova Scotian family members and myself, as previously stated, resided in a community where the population was predominately white. We were not taught in school about the history of our ancestors and historical individuals of African descent. The majority of the individuals I associated with were non-African Nova Scotians, and those who were of the same descent as myself were also not cognizant of all the aspects of our culture. During my first and third year in university I had an African Nova Scotian roommate. My roommate, in addition to other individuals of African descent who I met during the early years of university, were major influences in my life in relation to learning more about myself, my cultural identity and history.

Following the completion of my first university degree, Bachelor of Arts, I continued my educational pursuit and was accepted into the Bachelor of Social Work Program at the same university.

As a student enrolled in a university program that teaches social work theories in relation to making positive changes in society, I expected that racism and prejudice would not be blatant in this learning environment. Unfortunately, this was not the case. One of a few incidents that I can vividly recall was when a white professor ended a class early because his interpretation of a situation between students in the class was that it was becoming a racial issue. The situation commenced when another African Nova Scotian student and I were whispering comments to each other about a video that we were watching during the class. The incident precipitated a white student in the class yelling at us, "Why don't you guys be quiet or something. We can't hear." The comment made by the white student escalated into a verbal dispute between her and another white student and the African student and myself. The comment and reaction to the incident by the professor was inappropriate and indeed probably racist; however, he never apologized.

The details, accurate or inaccurate, regarding that incident became the topic of conversation for many of the students at the School of Social Work. There was a period that the African and white students were not socializing with each other because of the situation that resulted in the conflict between two African and two white students. At that point, the situation had developed into a racial issue. In an attempt to resolve this matter, some of the African students, including myself, met with the Director of the School, who was white. The Director listened to the concerns conveyed by us, but did not provide us with an update respecting if and how the matter was dealt with, especially the action of the professor involved. There were also other incidents of racism that were encountered by African students during the completion of my Bachelor of Social Work degree, but this one stands out as particularly troubling.

Despite the challenges with racism, the School of Social Work also provided me with a number of positive life experiences. The support system available to new African students in the program, from African students close to completion of the program, was invaluable. During my second year at the school I joined the Association of Black Social Workers, which is still today a support system for me in my personal and professional life.

In addition to the support system developed while a student at the Maritime School of Social Work, another positive experience was the field placements I completed during my Bachelor of Social Work Degree. My first field placement was in an African Nova Scotian community assisting young adults who were seeking employment. My field supervisor for this placement was an African Nova Scotian female who provided me with ongoing support through her mentorship. Today this individual remains as a positive role model and support in all the aspects of my life.

My second field placement was with the Department of Community Services, Children and Family Services. At the time of my field placement, I was a casual employee with the Department of Community Services, Foster Care Program. I used this position as an opportunity to recruit and support the African foster parents involved in the child protection system. My field supervisor was also African Nova Scotian and was a permanent employee of the Department of Community Services. This individual has influenced me significantly since I first became involved with her at a professional level. She is a role model to me and many other African social workers. She has been a support to me personally and professionally. She has made a number of significant changes in the social work community and the Department of Community Services that have assisted members of the African Nova Scotian communities. There were times during my field placement when I had a number of responsibilities in my life and wanted to delay the completion of my Bachelor of Social Work degree. My field placement supervisor encouraged me to continue and finish this degree during the same year, while providing me with what I considered to be an immense amount of support.

The field placement with the Foster Care Program assisted the Department of Community Services with recruitment of additional African foster families, provided a support system for the existing African foster families and provided them with training opportunities in an environment where they experienced a level of comfort and support. The training opportunities were facilitated by African professionals and held in the African Nova Scotian communities.

During my early years as an employee with the Department of Community Services, I was unaware of white children being placed in African foster homes. Within the last five years, employees within the Department of Community Services, through education and conversations with African professionals, have commenced placing white children in African foster homes. Prior to this change in the social workers' practices, it was common for them to place African children in non-African foster homes. Within the last three years, the Department of Community Services contracted the present Director of the School of Social Work, who is an African Nova Scotian female, to implement and train the Foster Care and Adoption Programs' social workers in the use of a culturally appropriate assessment tool to determine if the foster and adoptive parents have the cultural competence to provide placements for children of a different cultural background.

Following the completion of my second field placement I graduated with a Bachelor of Social Work degree. Having this degree was not sufficient, as I realized that if I wanted to advance in my career as an African Nova Scotian female, I had to pursue a further level of education. I also wanted to make some changes within the Department of Community Services for members of the African Nova Scotian communities and be a role model to other employees, African and non-African, within the field of social work. The two African Nova Scotians in management positions within the Department of Community Services in the Central Region of Nova Scotia are role models and an excellent support system for me; therefore, my goal is to follow their career paths.

The same year that I was accepted into the Maritime School of Social Work, Master of Social Work degree program, I was offered and accepted an Acting Casework Supervisor position with the Department of Community Services, Children and Family Services. Today I am a permanent casework supervisor and my plan is to strive toward further advancement within the Department of Community Services.

There was a time in my professional life that I considered leaving the field of child protection and pursuing a career as a clinical social worker. During this time, I was enrolled in the Master of Social Work program and arranged to complete a field placement in the area of mental health. I arranged to complete my field placement at a Child Play Therapy office. The positive aspect of this field placement was that I had a chance to gain a knowledge base about play therapy with children and conduct therapy sessions with two African Nova Scotian children. In Nova Scotia there are no certified African play therapists.

This field placement made me realize that there is definitely a need for African social workers and psychologists to be trained in this field. Although the therapist who was my field supervisor had been a certified play therapist for several years, she lacked skills in the area of cultural competence. There were only two culturally appropriate toys (for example, dolls) in her office; further-more, there were no books and pictures representative of different cultural backgrounds in her office. There were also a few occasions when I asked her cultural questions in relation to children she was involved in a therapeutic relationship with, but she was unable to answer the questions. It is imperative that therapists working with clients from different cultural backgrounds take time during their careers to enhance their level of cultural competence if they want the clients to benefit from the therapeutic processes.

Part of this chapter has focused on my field placement while a student at the Maritime School of Social Work. I want to also focus on the courses I was enrolled in at the school. One of my favourite courses, because of the positive learning experience, was Africentric Perspectives in Social Work, which was taught by the present Director of the School who is African Nova Scotian. There were four students registered in this course. The students consisted of another African Nova Scotian female, an East Indian female and a white female. All the students conveyed to each other and the professor the level of comfort we felt during attendance of this course, which allowed us to openly communicate our opinions pertaining to all the issues discussed. My positive opinion regard-ing this learning experience for myself and possibly the other stu-dents was because we had an African Nova Scotian professor who encouraged us to share our feelings and appeared to be open to lis-tening to all our opinions without casting judgements.

During this course we explored how to implement an Afric-entric Model of Social Work Practice in our fields of practice. All the students conveyed that there were individuals in our places of employment who assumed that an Africentric Model of Social Work Practice could only be used with members of African com-munities. The professor assisted the students with techniques that could be used to educate our colleagues and community members, African and non-African, about the benefits of utilizing an Afri-centric Model of Social Work Practice with individuals from differ-ent cultural backgrounds.

My first experience of applying an Africentric Model of Social Work Practice was with an African Nova Scotian family that I was involved with who had trust issues in relation to social workers, especially African social workers. The adults in this family were concerned with the issue of confidentiality because the African community in the Central Region of Nova Scotia was small. Furthermore, because of the internalized racism, the adults believed that non-African social workers were more qualified than African social workers. I implemented several social work theories/practices to engage the members of this family and to elicit their cooperation with the child protection intervention, but my attempts were unsuccessful. The professor of the Africentric Social Work course suggested that I convene an extended family meeting that included the clients, and members of their family who were interested in working with them and the child protection professionals, to alleviate the agency's concerns. This model of social work practice encompasses components of the Africentric Model of Social Work Practice. This social work framework was successful in engaging the clients to cooperate with the agency's case plan to address the concerns that resulted in child protection involvement with them and their children.

As a casework supervisor in the field of child protection, I encourage my colleagues, especially the staff I supervise, to utilize an Africentric Model of Social Work in their daily practice. Presently my staff present as culturally competent when working with clients from different cultural backgrounds; however, as their supervisor I also have a responsibility to ensure that they adhere to this practice. I think there needs to be ongoing training for social workers to ensure that they are utilizing culturally appropriate models of social work practice, such as Anti-Oppressive and Africentric Models of Social Work Practices.

It is imperative that organizations who employ professionals in the human service and social work fields continue to ensure that their staff are trained to meet the needs of the clients they serve, in a culturally competent manner. As a casework supervisor in the social work field, I can have an influence to a certain degree with encouraging senior management and front-line staff to ensure that they are culturally competent. This task does not come without struggles, because I am one member who is of African descent in an organization predominately of white people but this will not deter me from ensuring this task is achieved.

In closing, I would like to express a few words of advice for present and future African social workers. Rely on other African social workers, community members and your church/spirituality for support. Things will not always be easy in life; you will encounter various struggles. However, God does not place upon you things that you are not capable of handling. Never give up on your goals in life and remember that you can always make a difference in the lives of others. As the African proverb states, "It takes a village to raise a child" and many children follow in the footsteps of their elders and mentors.

Chapter 7

A Vision of Social Work

Maxine Colley Wongus

I grew up in East Preston. I guess I knew everybody in the area because they were mainly my aunts, uncles and cousins. Everybody was related and everybody was Black. My parents were not my biological parents; I was adopted by my godparents. My birth mother gave me up when I was a year old and she moved away to Toronto. My birth mother was very poor and I understood that she lived under very inadequate conditions, and I became very sick. I was sick a lot and she felt she couldn't care for me anymore and asked them to take me. That was my understanding and then she moved away to try to get work. My older brother was my adopted parents' biological child, and my younger brother was actually a nephew of my mom's and his mother was somewhat in the same situation as my mother. He is actually like my cousin, but my brother by adoption. It all felt quite normal as we were related, and all of us were Black. I never lived around any other culture until we moved to Montreal when I was ten years old.

In East Preston it was a comfortable feeling because even though your parents might not be around when you went to school, somewhere in the neighbourhood someone was watching out for you and paying attention to what you were doing and telling you right from wrong. Sometimes you didn't appreciate it. You knew that if you did something wrong that you didn't think was all that bad, someone saw you and would tell your mother or your father and you'd get in trouble. When I look back it was comforting to know that it was a safe environment. You could walk down the road and you didn't have to worry about any kidnappers or anybody trying to hurt you because people were always on the lookout for the children, keeping an eye on them, whether it was their children or somebody else's children. There was that connection there.

Church was very important and our mother made sure we went to church and to Sunday school. There was a strong sense of spirituality. You were taught to honour your parents and all adults, especially seniors. People always looked out for one another and helped one another out. It wasn't something that you had to be told, it was something that you knew.

I remember how my mother and aunt used to get together and we'd go pick berries. The women went together and did things together. At one time my mother was a stay-at-home mom and then we'd pick berries and we went as a group. If people didn't have a lot of money, which we didn't, I wasn't aware that things were tough sometimes because we always had lots to eat. A lot of my uncles and close friends were farmers or they drove a truck that would pick up the excess vegetables from stores or from the bakery. They would keep some food for themselves and distribute the rest to friends and family who needed it. People grew livestock so they had cows and you could get things at a minimum price. Sundays were very festive. We had big events like baptisms and people went to visit one other. People would feed large numbers of people and there wasn't any worry as to how much you were eating. It was always a sit-down supper and the family ate together. The father was considered the head of the household.

When I went to Montreal there were all kinds of nationalities, and that was my exposure to other cultures. When I first moved there, my best friend was a French girl and there was actually another Black girl who lived next door to me and only a few of us spoke English because virtually everybody spoke French. The area where I lived was the poorer side of town and eventually it seemed like the French people moved out and it was just all English speakers left. Nonetheless, you were exposed to other nationalities. People came from other countries to live there. That was also a good experience for me because I was always very eager to learn new things, meet other people and hear new languages. All that part didn't bother me, but I still came across racism.

When I went to school in East Preston, it was segregated but when I went to Montreal the schools had all different nationalities and the segregation was between Protestants and Roman Catholics, and I went to a Protestant School. At the time I went to school in East Preston the school teachers were mostly Black. There were a couple of white teachers but I don't think they were there when I was there. Maybe they were but I don't remember seeing them. Again, it was accepted and I didn't think about having white teachers or anything. It was just that you had those teachers and that was your life. It was in Montreal that I had my first experience of having white teachers and I didn't have any Black teachers until I went to high school.

In the elementary school in Montreal I experienced racism from the teachers. I knew it, but I wasn't quite sure. In retrospect I am sure of it. I used to try and figure it out all on my own. I sometimes wondered if the teacher picked on all Black kids. There weren't a whole lot of Black kids there to pick on, but I used to try to think it through and sometimes I thought maybe it was just me or I would think it was the Black kids. We were either kind of ignored or, in my case, yelled at more or got into trouble for something that another child might not get in trouble for at all because the teacher would just say to them, "Now you know, don't do that again." If you did the same thing you would be embarrassed in front of the whole class and asked, "Why did you do that? Are you stupid or something?"

You didn't go home and tell your parents because, first of all, you were made to feel like you had done something wrong and if you told your parents naturally you would get into more trouble. So you just put up with whatever, and tried to be quiet and behave as best you could so that the teacher would not bother you. I had a few teachers that I feel were racist.

I really am not sure at what stage of my life I gave racism a name. I don't know, because we never talked about it then. It probably wasn't till high school that I really put words to it. I also had another experience with racism, besides my experiences with the teachers. There was a boy who lived near me who called me "nigger black" one time, and it was so shocking because no one had ever said that to me in East Preston. You were treated a little different, but you weren't called names. He used to try to beat up my little brother, so I had to fight with him and then he called me nigger.

Another time, I had a Chinese friend and I was carrying on with her. We were walking home from school and I was teasing her. I took her school bag from her and I was pretending that I was walking away with her school bag. It turned out that I was right in front of her house and her father came out yelling, and I brought the school bag back. The next day she told me her father told her not to play with me because people like me were bad. I knew she meant Black people. But she was okay. We still played together at school but she told me what her father said so I knew that Chinese people could also be racist against us.

There was a lot of turmoil in the family and my father and mother separated. I don't remember what grade I was in, perhaps in junior high. My mother took my brother and me, and we went to live somewhere else, but still it was the same setup. We were sharing someone's house. We had what nowadays would be called a bachelor room. We didn't even have a bedroom; we just had a curtain up to separate the living area from the bedroom. My mother had to work and I was in charge of the house when she went. I think she was home in the mornings when my brother and I went to school. I took him to school. When I came home at night she was already gone to work, and it was my job to make supper and get him ready for bed and make sure the house was cleaned. I must have been twelve when my mother, my brother and I moved out.

As a pre-teen and teenager I felt my mother was very strict and so I went to live with my father. I was with him for a while and my mother asked me to come live with her again so I went back and lived with her. Then I was upset again and I went back to my father. I must have done that about four times. Finally, my mother moved back to East Preston and I stayed with my father in Montreal, but I moved down to Nova Scotia when I was in grade eleven. I came to live with Mom and he stayed in Montreal. My father came back maybe a year later around the time when I was finishing high school. During my first year at the university I again went to live with my father.

It was when I moved back to Nova Scotia that racism became clear to me. I really noticed the difference between being Black and white. Firstly, you hardly saw any other nationalities and you didn't really associate with anybody else. Once you lived out here, the school had Black and white children but I don't remember seeing anybody else really. I had one Indian teacher, but really nobody of colour. I felt like an outsider at the school. I didn't feel right, I didn't fit in. It wasn't so bad that first year because I had all my girlfriends and they took me back. We were close but in spite of that closeness we had different interests.

Some of my girlfriends were more interested in guys, or in drinking, or smoking and those weren't my interests. I couldn't hang out with them at school too much. They had their own group that they chatted with and with whom they hung out. A lot of the times I found myself just being by myself and I'd go to the library or eat my lunch right quick. One of my close friends had moved into town and that really cut me off. She was really my best friend and she had two other friends and while she was there we were all good, but when she left I had nothing in common with them, so I really felt like I was by myself.

I'd go to school and just do my work and just managed to stay in. I don't know if I was depressed but I was going to quit school in grade eleven. I really didn't feel happy and I started to feel like

I was not getting anywhere. I was just not going to do anything. It felt as if my life had no purpose and I was getting ready to quit school in grade eleven. I went to the guidance counsellor and tried to find out what I could do as far as education or a job went. The guidance counsellor told me, "Well, you could go and take a cooking course" and "This is where you go." That was all the advice I got.

Even when I talked to my mother, because nobody in the family had graduated from high school before, she was sure I could get a job if I quit school if that was what I wanted. She said she would rather I didn't, but I could if I wanted. I thought about it and I was really going to quit. I don't know what changed my mind, but I did change my mind. I continued and I went back and did grade twelve. I found grade twelve was a better experience, but overall my high school experience is not something that I want to relive; it was not a good time for me. I got pregnant in grade twelve and had the baby in December, so I still managed to graduate high school. When it came time to go to university in September, I didn't bother going. I just stayed out of school for a year until I had my son and the next year I went to university.

I was nineteen when I went to Mount Saint Vincent University (MSVU), but I don't think I was focused enough. I did what I thought I wanted to do and I think I would have succeeded but, for some reason, I didn't believe I could succeed. For some reason, I decided to be a teacher and I started the program at MSVU in 1974. I really didn't know who to ask or how to get support or help. At the university it is a different way to study and a different way to do things and I just didn't know that. When I went, I tried to take a whole lot of courses in one year and failed many of them. I started to feel bad. It just felt like I wasn't getting anywhere. Then I went the second year and did so poorly that they asked me not to come back. So I went to work. I just didn't have the necessary support to succeed in university.

I took a student loan to go to university and it took me ten years to pay it off. I ran into so much debt. I had a bit of determination, so I got work and I worked for a couple of years, then I got married. We worked at different jobs. Then after my third child was born we broke up. I wasn't working because she has a disability and I didn't know anybody that I trusted to raise her while I went to work or school, so I stayed at home. I was on welfare when I stayed home, which was a big adjustment because I had always worked since I was sixteen – I did summer work and it was only those two years that I was home with my daughter that I didn't work. Then I met some nice people, who encouraged me and helped to ease me back into the work force. I worked at community agencies in the human service fields and that helped me to start thinking about what I wanted to do with my life. Then I decided to go back to university to study social work.

All of my life experiences – having a child with a disability and the need for a good permanent job – led me to decide to become a social worker. In addition, I was also influenced by people who I worked with in the community agencies. As poor as my parents were, they were not on welfare; it was just not an option. I always thought that being on welfare was a shameful thing. I felt that as a good healthy person, there was no reason for me to stay on welfare. My experience as a single mother also made me want to help other women break the cycle of dependency.

I applied and was accepted in the undergraduate program at the Maritime School of Social Work at Dalhousie University. It took me three and a half years because I was able to transfer my credits, and I went full-time. At the time, my two youngest children were in day care and the oldest was in school. I went to classes during the day, was with them at night, and then studied when they went to bed. I was dead tired all the time and I had no social life. The only thing I had was church. When I was in my last year of study my partner and I got back together. He was self-employed and working at home, so he was there when the children got in from school, and I continued with my studies.

After I graduated, I tried applying for jobs and became very discouraged because I went to some of those same places that I had gone for help and was repeatedly told, "You don't have enough experience." The only time I managed to get a position was when the job description said they were looking for an African Canadian, so I benefited from affirmative action, but that full-time job I sought was an illusion.

After getting my Bachelor's degree in social work I worked in a number of community-based agencies. Eventually I got a full-time position with a quasi government agency, and they too had recruited a visible minority person. I worked there for ten years. When I left there I went to a government department in a term position, which I also used as a placement (I was completing my MSW at that time).

The ten years with the quasi government agency as a full-time employee was a stressful time. My manager was psychologically abusive, and I felt constantly attacked and harassed. I could not do the job the way I felt it should be done, and near the end I felt that everything I did was wrong. It nearly destroyed me and my confidence in my own abilities. Although it was difficult to give up a full-time job for a term position, I felt that my mental health could not cope with the problems there anymore.

From there I went to the government department, and although I thought I was doing well, my supervisor led others to believe that I was not capable of handling the job. I went from one term position to another, with two degrees in social work, and it was quite stressful. I worked there for almost four years but I never got a permanent position.

Last year, a term position came up in health care, where I am presently working, and I am hopeful that now I will get a permanent position. When I finished university I expected to get a permanent position and I thought I was going to have a career but all this bouncing around gets me down. I may as well have been a garbage collector because what was the use of going to university, spending all of that money, borrowing all of that money from Student Loans, being in debt for years and years?

I really feel angry and discouraged. How do we encourage our children to go to university? I encourage mine to a point, but then I tell them, see if you can find a career in something that is marketable then do it because you might go to university and it may not mean anything after borrowing so much money. I encourage them, but on the other hand I'm saying well, I don't want them to think that university is the "be all end all" because it isn't.

Maybe part of the problem is the fact that this is Nova Scotia. I also tell them that if you feel that you want to move away and try somewhere else out there, do that, because every place is not like here. I find that in Nova Scotia there is still a lot of racism. It's not just a person; it's the whole way they do things in different institutions. When I was with the government department people looked to me as some kind of expert on any issue dealing with Black people because usually, you're the only Black person there and so you're supposed to know everything. They also wanted to know who the leader of the Black community was and so on. It is a problem when you are expected to know how Black people feel all the time or when you're supposed to know everything about every Black person or to know every Black person.

I find the racism is even worse in school. For instance, I don't feel that the teachers really encourage my teenage son enough. The teachers spend so much time policing that they can't even try to look for the children's potential. I find my son is turned off school and we're having a real struggle, trying to keep him interested and keep him enthusiastic to keep going.

I believe parents have given up too much of their rights and that is one of the issues I used to encounter while working with the parents in the child welfare system. I realize I'm going in there with the power and I'm saying, "You do this, this, and this or your children are going to be taken from you or I have to keep coming back and telling you how to parent your children." On the other hand, my belief is that you need to stand up and say I'm the parent and I'm going to raise my child, and give a little bit of a fight. In actuality, if a person gives too much fight then we say that person is non-cooperative or resistant. I never used that word with clients because I like to try and see what the parents' beliefs are, and I believe that a parent should be able to be stern. I think the state should have as little involvement as possible. So even though I'm there as a state worker, I feel better when the parent tells me, "This is how I'm going to do it" or "this is what I believe," rather than simply agreeing with everything that's dictated to them.

We say, we're going to do everything, take the least intrusive measure, we're doing the least intrusive thing, and in some situations it has to do with money and all the parents need is maybe some extra resources or some extra money to do certain things for the child or with the child that would maybe relieve the family of stress or just make things work better. Then the agency would say, "We're not spending any more money in that area." They are allowed so many visits to the psychiatrist or we got so much money to spend for day care and once that is gone that is it. I had a few experiences like that and it really bothered me because you are saying two conflicting things. We're telling the parent to do everything and cooperate with us, and then when it looks like they're spending too much money we pull services. Then if they run into a problem with the child we're there threatening to take the child.

It was only when I became involved with the Association of Black Social Workers that I started to really face racism head-on and to talk about it and realize what was happening to me was largely due to racism. The ABSW gave me the environment to express some of the pain I experienced. I was really pleased to join and I always felt better knowing that other social workers were dealing with some of the same things that I was experiencing.

When I feel that I'm not doing a good job as a social worker they help me realize I may have some problem, but really it's not just me; it could be the system and there is racism at play. It's been a great source of support and I really needed it, especially when I was being harassed in the full-time job. I used to come to so many meetings saying, "Please, help me find a job because I've got to get out of here." They were very supportive. I'm looking forward to us getting our mentoring program started because I think that would be a good thing. Not everyone functions well in a group. Although we've got the ABSW there for support, sometimes a person may benefit more from having a one-on-one support system in place.

I think I reached my goal only because I had a different vision of what being a social worker is because social work is so linked to politics and money. It is definitely not what I thought it was and it's not what I set out to do. I didn't plan to be the police and I didn't plan to have to budget and have to worry about spending and so on.

I still want to do social work; I enjoy social work when I am doing it. I've sometimes had to do some other different things outside of my actual job because the work can be so discouraging at times. I hate being an agent of social control, but I enjoy doing workshops and working for change. ABSW used to do anti-racism workshops at the School of Social Work. I really enjoyed that, and I have taken part in some health and racism awareness workshops and done some vigils and work around family violence. Such things make me feel satisfied that I am doing social work. If it was just my day-to-day work, I would not feel satisfied and I would feel like I haven't really accomplished anything much. It is mainly these community projects that keep me going, and feeling good about being a social worker. I am thankful for ABSW and the strong links that I have with my community, for these help to sustain me and keep me motivated to do good social work in my workplace.

Chapter 8

The Skin I'm In

Lois Fairfax

The skin I'm in has exposed me to many pivotal experiences throughout my life journey. My current stop on this journey is a place of acceptance, peacefulness and spirituality.

Throughout my social work career I have incorporated a calm, non-judgemental approach with keen listening skills to form strong working relationships with many difficult clients. My social work experience has been gained through eight years working in child welfare and seven years in children's mental health. Being a visible minority and experiencing racism in countless forms has led me to set a high standard of acceptance of others. This in particular applies to the clients that I am assigned to work with. As a result of my ability to establish strong working relationships, a pattern emerged, in that I tended to receive the more contentious cases. I learned very early in life that giving others the ability to express themselves and to be understood was essential to establishing strong relationships. That proved invaluable, especially in child welfare, where, as a mandated service, many of my clientele did not invite me to become involved with their families.

While officially starting my social work career in 1989, my social consciousness has been intact for as long as I can remember. Growing up a member of Nova Scotia's Black community in a family where I was the youngest of six meant that I also had five unique perspectives to learn from. The perspectives of my siblings, in addition to those of my parents, made family my first classroom. The need to obtain higher education was ingrained very early in life as it was viewed as a means to self-sufficiency, equality and new experiences, the ultimate goal being that those new experiences would create more visibility, opportunities and acceptance of Blacks. It was known that there were systemic barriers to obtaining higher education and that any decision made regarding school was never without input from our parents. So despite a lack of role models in the school system, the expectations set by my family guided me in setting high standards for myself.

My father being one of the community's leaders and my mother's strong social conscience meant that social awareness was genetic. Social awareness took the form of understanding the plight of the poor versus the wealthy; the sick and the homeless; systemic barriers; discrimination based on race, colour, gender and sexual orientation. Social awareness also meant understanding the subtleties by which things are conveyed. After all, while our American neighbour's form of racism was and is very blatant and overt, Canada's was and is not always that obvious. This meant that you had to work harder at being conscious of what was occurring around you. So while I can recall having acquaintances in elementary and junior high school who were allowed to have a "Black friend" as long as it was not a boy, or those who required me to wait outside their home while they ran inside for something, and the public outcry when a Black teen was cast in the lead role of *Jesus Christ – Superstar* at my siblings' high school, it was always apparent to me what the real issues were. Whether the more subtle systemic racism or the overt form, the school system (Guidance Department in particular) was notorious for channelling Black students into non-academic courses, hence eliminating their ability to pursue higher education.

I quickly realized early in life that the next step after recognizing racism was deciding what your response was going to be. Throughout my life journey I used to harbour such contempt for the racial inequalities I observed or experienced personally. That contempt has evolved over time with maturity and self-growth into an acceptance of the reality of racism, and seeing it as an opportunity to educate where possible. Utilizing the opportunity to educate under such difficult circumstances also meant seizing the moment, as timing is essential.

I learned the value of timing during an incident while completing my Bachelor of Social Work degree. During the summer school break of my second year in the program, I had gotten an exciting job at the Canada Employment Centre for Students. I remember that after finishing my Bachelor of Arts degree and not having a clear career focus, I had decided to pursue social work after many talks with Dr. Wanda Thomas Bernard. Given the mistrust of the career counselling offered in the school system to Blacks and the limited Black educators at the university level, it was essential to seek out a role model you could identify with. So by my second year of study in social work, I felt excited about the program and the summer job I had secured.

While on lunch break from the Employment Centre, I was en route to meet someone when I passed two Caucasian men on the sidewalk. At the moment of our passing one of the men stopped and stated to the other man in a loud voice that "it had been a long time since he rode a nigger." I stopped in shock and disbelief. I looked at the man and asked, "What did you say?" Hoping that I had heard wrong, I waited for a reply when the men approached me. My shock and disbelief changed to the most intensive feeling of fear that, to this date, I have only felt at one other time in my life. That adrenaline rush of fear caused me to run. That incident used to replay in my thoughts constantly after it occurred.

I would have loved to know what was in that man's thoughts to have said something so derogatory. I would also wonder if there was some way I could have prevented the comment. After rationalizing that one cannot prevent ignorance in others and the importance of not jeopardizing one's safety, the incident lost its impact on me. However, I vowed that from that incident on, I would never be left speechless or running again when dealing with racism.

When I was attending the Maritime School of Social Work I never could have imagined that the formal education I was receiving would be put into practice in such a culturally diverse city as Toronto. However, as regional disparity would have it, social work jobs in the Maritimes were limited, so like many Maritimers before me, I had to leave to find a full-time job in my field elsewhere. Systemic racism also factored into this phase of my life when, as a new graduate eager to start my social work career, I was only able to secure the odd contract here in Nova Scotia. There was no employment equity policy in place at the time and it was rare that Blacks (or other visible minorities) accessed the permanent positions. I too became part of the brain drain of Nova Scotian professionals to other provinces, which also meant that the local communities could not benefit from their investment in future role models for the next generation. Although many returned to Nova Scotia after obtaining a few years of experience, many such as myself did not. While Nova Scotia is culturally diverse, it is not nearly on the same scale of the diversity I experience in Toronto.

I immediately fell in love with the diversity of the communities. It was equally exciting to find that amongst the Black community the world was represented, with those of Caribbean descent having the largest representation. That was quite different from my community in Nova Scotia where Blacks are referenced as an "indigenous group," given the community was first inhabited in 1782 and it is common to date your ancestors back six or eight generations. Given the long history of the Blacks in the Maritimes, we do not have a recognizable accent, which can become an issue in a city where each Black group had their own distinguishable sound.

This first became apparent to me while working in child welfare where I was frequently asked to show my identification "to verify that I was the person spoken to on the phone." While this request seemed perfectly harmless, I later realized my other colleagues were seldom requested to show their identification. A similar incident occurred after apprehending a child and accessing a foster home placement. The foster mother, with whom I had spoken many times, was shocked to open her front door and find a Black social worker. In an attempt to explain her look of disbelief, the foster mother asked me if I have ever talked with someone on the phone and envisioned what he or she looked like.

Finally, I thought to myself, someone honest enough to admit they prejudged the sound of my voice as not belonging to a person of colour. I concurred with the foster mother that indeed I had spoken with people on the phone and envisioned what they looked like. The foster mother then proceeded to say that "in speaking with me, I sounded as though I was tall"! I told the foster mother that I disagreed, as you cannot attribute a sound to one's height. I told her what I believed – that her look of disbelief was a reaction to finding a person of colour at her door when she thought she was speaking with someone else. The foster mother, while embarrassed, agreed. This also presented an opportunity to address whether or not she would have any difficulty in working with me, given her initial response. As mentioned, timing is essential when dealing with racial biases. It has been my experience that if you second-guess yourself and attempt to address a bias at a later time, it is not effective.

Practising social work in the Toronto area has also meant having easy access to great professional development opportunities. With the current industry buzz looking at "Best Practices," I believe it is equally important to highlight self-care. Health professionals have a poor track record in this area yet it is vitally important. Social workers can use analysis, clinical supervision or other means to process their use of self in the therapeutic relationships they form. However, it may not be so straightforward for Black social workers as our race and ethnicity may factor into the dynamics and complicate things. I can remember participating in a variety of different training seminars that looked at "transference and counter transference," "establishing the therapeutic alliance," and "the use of self in therapy." I would be aware of not only my own experiences, but some of the experiences of other Black social workers who chose not to offer their stories in training. It has been my experience that as Black social workers we seek out one another and process the difficult dynamics we find ourselves in, as opposed to utilizing the more traditional means like clinical supervision.

The last time I utilized the more traditional means of looking at a difficult therapeutic alliance was during my graduate program at the University of Toronto. I was doing my social work practicum in family therapy at an agency outside Toronto that was not very culturally diverse. It was agreed that, as an experienced social worker, I would work with about four to six families. During clinical supervision, my field instructor queried about two families who were not consistent in utilizing their sessions.

For some time I had wondered whether utilizing treatment from a visible minority could be a factor for them. In one of the families, the mother refused to attend after the first session but the father continued coming with his sons. In the other family, appointments were scheduled and not attended. What was consistent, however, was the parents' reaction to me upon our first meeting. It was apparent that they were surprised that I was Black. After exhausting all possibilities as to what was going on in the sessions and using videotape, I offered my impressions on the transference and possible racial angle for discussion.

My field instructor became defensive and asked what proof I had. I was then asked whether I was getting any help for "my problem." My field instructor's response resulted in my decision to not jeopardize my graduate degree by raising all of the relevant clinical dynamics that I felt may be occurring. Despite having a faculty advisor, and a practicum liaison person, the task of selling my clinical viewpoint, including the cultural perspective, seemed too arduous to pursue. I realized that there was no safe space in the academic arena for me to address this issue. I was able to later process this through consultation with another Black social worker.

While revealing oneself is risky, factoring in racial themes that may or may not be obvious only further complicates things. That is why many Black social workers do not expose that side of their clinical work. In Toronto we do not have an Association of Black

Social Workers as our counterparts do in Halifax. While there have been attempts to organize a chapter locally, that has not occurred to date, and has proven to be a challenging task given the sheer geography of Toronto as just one of the major obstacles to be overcome. Having a body where we can address these issues and educate others will hopefully be a reality at some time in the future. Perhaps the writing of this book may be the catalyst for starting such an organization.

Currently, I am a new (six months) social work supervisor at a children's mental health agency outside Toronto. In that capacity I also maintain a small caseload providing individual, couple and/or family therapy. I co-facilitate a women's therapy group as well. My social work practice is heavily grounded in theories pertaining to ethnic sensitive social work practice, feminist theory, systems theory, and cognitive behavioural therapy. Other approaches I have used in my clinical work include solution-focused, brief therapy, narrative therapy, and expressive art therapy. My current interest is in the literature on mindfulness and incorporating it into clinical practice. Mindfulness is a form of concentration that facilitates heightened awareness of thoughts, emotions and behaviours. It is used in social work practice to reduce stress, anxiety and depression, and to improve physical and emotional functioning. Specific mindfulness techniques can empower individuals to gain control over their thoughts and behaviours.

Being a supervisor has brought my professional journey full circle in that I now have the responsibility to provide clinical guidance and understanding to my staff. I am empowered to know that my professional and life experiences have culminated in this new opportunity for me to relate to my fellow colleagues on a variety of levels. As there are not a large number of social worker supervisors who are visible minorities in children's mental health, I have set my bar of excellence high to ensure I perform above average in fulfilling the requirements of the job. In that way I hopefully may be creating opportunities for others.

After receiving the supervisory position, I felt an initial fright as the enormity of my new responsibilities became apparent. Then

I realized that by drawing on the professional experiences I had, combined with learning the nuances of management and maintaining the agency's goals and focus, this position is a natural progression for me.

I attended training for new supervisors recently and found comfort in knowing my initial fears were common amongst other new supervisors. Some of the shared challenges identified were being promoted in an agency where you formerly were a clinician and now you have to supervise your former colleagues or having my situation of maintaining a few clients in addition to supervising. While it can be perceived that I am "wearing two hats," establishing myself in the new role has been essential. Another shared challenge was the writing of evaluations. This was related to the confidence we had in our own ability to rate the performance of staff.

As I participated in this training it became apparent how my experiences would be drawn upon to guide me in facing the challenging aspects of my new position. Staying current with the research and literature on social work trends and practices is an additional task that I look forward to doing so that I can share this knowledge. The last six months, while challenging, have gone very well. I have finished my probationary period and am looking forward to further growth in this role.

The skin I'm in has been both challenging and rewarding as I learned to navigate my way in the social work profession. The journey continues as I creatively use acts of racism as opportunities to educate others.

Chapter 9

The Past That Influenced My Path

Wanda Taylor

As social workers we are often challenged to the limit in our daily lives, personally, morally, and emotionally. It is our inner strength, spiritual beliefs, and life experiences that allow us to remain grounded most times. But even we reach limits. It is what we learn and how we deal with these situations that allow us to honour our humanness. And it is because of this I would like to share my story.

I was raised in a small Black community as the youngest of seven children. My mother was a single woman who never married. She was born in the midst of the Depression when poverty was a way of life. People learned to do a lot with very little. My mother learned to do the same. People then arose before the sun and toiled long and hard to provide for their families. People travelled miles into town to work and to sell what they had harvested from the land, just to put food on their tables.

In the community where I was raised, families were often quite large. It was not uncommon in those days for families to have ten, fifteen, or even twenty children. This was a mixed blessing. It meant more mouths to feed, but as the children grew older, to their parents, it also meant more hands to help out and more members to contribute to the family's welfare. The down side to this was that children were often removed from school early in order to contribute their share. In many cases, education was sacrificed.

My mother, who was the youngest of fifteen, left school in grade five. Throughout her life and as she raised her children alone, she worked in jobs that required her to work hard and she received little pay. She, like many others in her situation, was stigmatized as a poor, Black, single mother, and she had to deal with racism, classism and sexism, and the intersection of these oppressions in her life. Unfortunately, this meant that she stood out. She was separated, orphaned by her community. This judgement extended beyond her community and into society as a whole. There was little support or services made available to her.

What societal services that were in place to assist were like thieves to the human soul, taking away her only possession: her dignity. Women in her situation were not respected. They were seen as the undeserving poor, having created their own plight. Service providers made them feel as though they had carved their own paths to poverty and struggle by choosing to bear children out of wedlock. They were bound to shame as the leaders of their families, especially those who found themselves forced to rely on society's welfare system for financial support. This hurt did not come without a price. The pains of low self-esteem, feeling devalued and unworthy, encircled our family structure.

Also, there was fallout of having one parent who worked tirelessly around the clock to put food on the table for so many of us. There was little time for a quality, emotionally fulfilling, parent/child relationship. I remember as a child feeling very alone and neglected, even though I was surrounded by siblings. I craved for any bit of affection that happened to trickle down my way. My mother was never shown how to give and receive affection, and therefore was at a loss to show it or teach it to her own children. For a woman who had suffered through such a painful and difficult childhood and adult life, she hardened her heart and her soul, even towards her children. She had little tolerance for the shortcomings of her children. Her use of corporal punishment was cruel, and her denial of love and affection dictated who her children were to become as adults.

As a child, I couldn't help but feel like I was a burden to her. I tried to be always obedient and always right. I thought that this effort would ease some of her hardships even though she spent very little time making me feel special or wanted. I felt she looked at her children and saw in our souls the source of all her deepest wounds and hurts. I felt she kept love and affection away from her children as a means of avoidance. I believe she tried not to give any more of herself, as she had already given of herself to so many people in her past that she felt hurt and betrayed deeply. As a child, I eventually felt emotionally deprived. I developed a perception of the unjust world around me, and began to seek out what I felt I needed to survive.

I feel there are decisions we all make in life based on our knowledge of the world, who we are and the experiences of our past. Each of these has an influence on which road we travel on our life's journey. My own past experiences have shaped who I am, what I believe, and why I chose the work that I do.

These thoughts bring me back to an experience of my past. I was separated from my family when my mother was in a serious car accident. The five youngest children were placed in the foster care system while my mother spent several months going through recovery. I was very young during this time, but I still have memories of being taken to a white foster home. During my time there, I remember being overwhelmed at the fact that my needs were being met in a way I had never experienced before. It wasn't that my mother was unwilling, but I believe she was unable to provide what I needed to thrive as a child. She did what she could with what she had, and with what was within her capabilities to provide. For me, however, it fell short of being adequate.

I remember being puzzled at the foster home when I observed a large bowl of juicy red grapes sitting out on the kitchen table. Having grapes in my home was a very rare luxury. I remembered that in my home, there were many nights when there was just nothing to eat, and that was my reality. Summertime was always my happiest time of year. All summer long I ate blueberries and strawberries and crab apples from the field. They were free, available, and plentiful. These are the only memories I have of feeling like my stomach was full. Seeing that bowl of grapes at the foster home just sitting out on the table, and being told that I could take as many as I wanted, was simply unheard of for me.

I often remember the story my brother still tells about my mother sending him to the corner store at nine years old to buy a loaf of bread. He recalls how he had received the worst beating of his life because he was so hungry, that he opened up the bread and ate it on the way home. By the time he returned, there were only a few slices left in the bottom of the bag. From our perspective he was punished for being hungry and that still bothers me. What message was sent to us as children, who had little control over our portion in life?

I was unable to give a voice to those feelings at such a young age, but am now able to look back, remember those feelings, and know that it was at that time I was discovering that I was a neglected, emotionally starved child. Within a year, I was returned to my mother, and my family was reunited. The older ones had since moved on and created separate lives for themselves. They seldom looked back. I believe they too at that time were stepping out into the world in search of emotional fulfillment, to relieve the empty void in their own souls.

As I grew older, I began to challenge what I had initially believed was going to be my way of life. The neglect I suffered carried on into my teen years. As a teenager, I was not provided with the support and the provisions of my physical and emotional needs that were integral to my success throughout those most difficult years. Necessities such as deodorant and sanitary pads were not provided for me, which I never understood. I was at that time unable to provide these things for myself. I was left to resort to the bare basics. This made my neglect so transparent that I was teased by my peers.

Along with my emotional and physical needs, my mother did not assist me on my academic journey. My mother never made one appearance at any sport or drama event that I was involved in during this time, even though I excelled greatly in these areas. Excellent grades and making the honour roll still did not grant me the emotional support and favour of my mother that I wanted and desperately needed. I, in turn, decided that I would venture out in search of the emotional fulfillment that my soul craved for. I needed to fill the hole that had taken up permanent residence deep within my soul.

As I grew on throughout my teen years, I began to find what I needed from "bad boys," the kinds of boyfriends a mother never wants her daughter to bring home. They were smooth, fast-talking charmers, who used you for what they needed to get from you, then tossed you aside to move on to the next conquest. My mother never questioned my choices, and never took an interest in wanting to meet the boys I was involved with. I received little guidance and support. As a result, I continued to fill that empty space in my soul temporarily over and over again, as "bad boys" charmed their way into my head and my heart. I had one parent who was not emotionally available. I could not introduce these boys to her. I could not share my feelings of being used by these boys with her. I could not seek out her help. I continued to seek out fulfillment in a series of short-lived, emotionally sick relationships. Each time I was left aching, but continued on a rampage to find the next one who would fill my void. I was simply too young and too naïve. I was unable to play their game.

This pattern magnified when at the age of seventeen I met the man who was to be my husband, and the father of my children. He, too, was trying to fill an emotional hole dug deep from his past experiences. It appeared that we completed each other. By the time I was eighteen, I was attending university and pregnant with my first child. Aborting the pregnancy never crossed my mind. There was no father to welcome my pregnancy, and no emotional or financial support from a partner. My then boyfriend continued to move on to other conquests. Soon after my first child was born, he returned and we reconciled. For me, it was the refilling of the emotional void that we both needed. Again, we completed each other.

Over the course of the next several years, we parted and reconciled many times. We continued to engage in toxic, repetitious destruction. In the midst of this, I gave birth to three more of his children, while he fathered four more for someone else. I followed the path of my mother, bearing children out of wedlock. I repeated her cycle and remained in this situation, because, for me, this was the only way I knew of to fill my deep, aching, emotional void. Being with this man at all costs was a lot less frightening than the unknown. The unknown was what else was out there for me to fill my void with.

Throughout the course of our fifteen-year relationship, the last seven of them as husband and wife, I worked with many children and families. I began volunteering with a non-profit agency. The director of this agency allowed me to become involved with so many different aspects of assisting families. I shadowed her when she went to women's homes, and provided counselling and support to them. Women who were poor, single, in crisis, or had lost their children though the child welfare system all sought assistance through this agency. In working with this agency, and with these women, I soon began to discover a different kind of fulfillment. I found a sense of joy in providing assistance and emotional support to families who were experiencing crisis in their lives. I found a sense of fulfillment in the unique way I could relate to them, and in the way they related to me.

Unfortunately, I was not in a place at that time in my life where I could distinguish this as a healthy fulfillment and my relationship with my partner as a dysfunctional one. Even though I realized that I was dealing with a man who was suffering from a mental illness, I'd had no teachings, no previous life examples to follow, and could not discern warnings of what danger lay ahead for me. My life's experiences provided me with nothing to store in my survival bank of life to draw from.

Throughout the course of my marital relationship, I continued to pursue paths that led me to opportunities to help families. I found work in the child care field for seven years and attended college for training in Early Childhood Education. I also worked in a volunteer capacity for Children's Aid, planning recognition events for foster parents and support to children in care. I also worked in a volunteer capacity with an association that assisted new immigrants to Canada, providing orientation and support. I quickly became drawn to the fulfillment I received from these types of opportunities to help others. I went on to obtain a degree in social work. This experience taught me to challenge the very beliefs I held firm to. It forced me to question and analyze my motivation for choosing the paths I chose. It helped me to think and to become informed. I felt enlightened and empowered.

This newfound sense of confidence and authority conflicted with my relationship with my husband. He often felt challenged, and became very defensive. This affected his mental state and began a chain of irrational behaviours. His thought process became clouded. He exercised improper judgement as it related to his children and family. This spiraled into the eventual breakdown of our family unit.

He brought into question my life as a Christian. I felt conflicted as an empowered woman. My Christian upbringing taught me that my union with my husband was ordained by God and, therefore, was to continue throughout the course of my lifetime. But I wanted out. Those teachings were in direct contradiction to what it meant for me to be empowered. My social work education taught me that we as women, and as an oppressed group in society, must stand up and demand to be seen and heard, and that my job as a social worker was to assist the oppressed members of society in becoming empowered.

Was I to abandon my strong religious beliefs and continue to be an empowered woman? Or was I to continue to work in the field helping other women, remaining in an emotionally abusive, emotionally sick relationship in obedience to my Christian values, even though they conflicted with what I was teaching to other women and families?

I agonized over my decision for several long months. Shortly after my graduation, I was offered a position as a child protection worker in Ontario. I packed up my clothes and my children and left my marriage. For months and months, I bore deep, deep guilt for abandoning the preaching of the Bible. I felt continually convicted by the scripture verses in Corinthians 1:10-11 that say, "To the married I give this command: A wife must not separate from her husband. But if she does, she must remain unmarried or else be reconciled to her husband."

I became unable to bear the emotional hole that quickly began to grow deeper. I was then without the dysfunctional emotional fulfillment we provided to each other. At that time, even distance couldn't spare me or separate me from the emotional sickness.

Within a year, I packed up and moved back. I felt I had abandoned my need to be an empowered woman, fulfilling my obligation to God by being a submissive wife. For another whole year, I bore the wrath of having left in the first place. My husband became even more emotionally abusive. I endured emotional suffering of the cruelest kind. He became constantly argumentative, accusatory, and continually unfaithful. All the urging and pleading in the world was not enough to convince him to get help for his illness. Still, I made the choice and I remained in the sickness with him.

This choice devastatingly conflicted with my work in the field, which was helping women and children to get out of situations similar to mine. Eventually, I realized that something had to give, and that I could not in good faith be honourable in my work while I lived this way. I thought about why I became a social worker, and the paths throughout my life that led me there. I started to see myself in my children. How could I give them the emotional strength and stability they deserved and that I craved for as a child, when I was being held captive in an emotional prison myself? And things weren't getting better.

This soul searching was my saving grace. I leaned more and more on the Bible, and I discovered that God did not want my children and me to live a life of suffering at the hands of this man. The Bible taught me that he, too, had an obligation to be obedient to God, and that he had failed in his life as a Christian to follow the teaching of the Bible as a husband and father. The scripture in Ephesians 5:22-28 says, "Husbands, love your wives, just as Christ loved the church and gave himself up for it, to make it holy, cleansing it by the washing with water through the word and to present it unto himself as a radiant church, without stain or wrinkle or any other blemish, but holy and blameless. In this same way, husbands ought to love their wives as their own bodies. He who loves his wife loves himself." Finally, in May of 2004, I filed for divorce. Sadly, this was not the end.

This decision to leave the relationship for good led to my husband's escalating violent and frightening behaviour. Even with an order from the court to stay away, he continued to harass me, smash windows, break into the home, cut wires, and everything else he could do to regain what he perceived to be a loss of control of our family, our children, and our home. The children were confused and afraid, as his actions became increasingly unpredictable.

Then, in September of 2004, he did the unthinkable. In a fit of rage, he got behind the wheel of an excavator and bulldozed our home shortly after the children and I left for school and work. Even a court order to remain away from the premises could not contain him from acting out his horrific plot for revenge. The children and I were left with no more than the clothes on our backs. I was quickly brought to my knees. How do you explain to a child that when you left for school this morning you had a home, but there is nothing for you to return to? To add to their pain, how do you then tell them that it was their own father who has done this? They have not spoken with him since. I believe that any form of relationship between him and the children would be harmful and unhealthy unless he received the help he desperately needs.

Each day following, as I worked in the child welfare field, listening to the sad stories of so many families, I was truly humbled. I felt like their stories were my stories. Their pain was also my pain. And their hope and resiliency, and will to overcome, would be mine as well. I stood determined not to be broken by this. I knew from within me that there is a reason for everything that happens to us in our lives. I believe there were signs long before I knew they were there.

I know now why I have chosen this field. I have a message to bring to others. It took me a long time to learn from the experiences of my life, but I have drawn strength from those experiences. I realized that I could have a relationship and an obedient walk with God, still follow his teachings, and still help women to become strengthened, confident, and empowered. I have learned to balance these roles, and feel that life's lessons have taught me precisely how to do so.

I believe that every path we take in life is for a purpose. Some follow the path that was chosen for them; others veer off to the right and to the left, in search of fulfillment. The tools you enter into the game with, those given to you by your parents, your past, your values, and your life experiences, determine what direction you will take on your path. It may take a lifetime for some to learn one huge life lesson, but the key to succeeding in life is to find that lesson in each phase of your life, good or bad, and use that lesson to carry you onto your next path.

My experience reminds me why I am in the helping profession. I use my lessons to effect change in others: in families who are going through crisis, in children who are crying out for help, and in those who are suffering. I can now use my life experiences to impart wisdom and knowledge to others and, most importantly, to my own children, as they begin to choose the paths for their lives.

There is much more work that needs to be done to assist women living in these types of situations, and a more united front for those out in the field working to effect change. Change not only comes from working with the women in these situations, but also from those who make the laws, as well as those whose job it is to enforce them. I have learned from personal experience that protocol and the implementation of newer, more efficient changes in the way domestic violence situations are handled have still fallen embarrassingly short of providing the much needed support and protection to women and families in crisis.

My experience has shown me that there are still very serious gaps within the justice system, and each of us as social workers, whether in the field or developing policies, has a responsibility to make ourselves aware of where these gaps lie. If we don't, then how do we know where to begin to effect change? I feel it is time to bring domestic violence back to the forefront of our agenda and not wait until we hear of another tragedy before we act. We have a responsibility as a professional body, and as members of what we consider to be a just society. Where we begin is not behind closed doors making policies, but out on the front line, hearing and documenting women's stories, and their experiences with the flaws in the system. We then need to sit at the table with those who are developing new protocols and making the laws, and those whose duty it is to enforce them. This way we can ensure there is fluidity and cohesiveness in the way in which society approaches and addresses these tragic situations.

It's time to reexamine our commitment to understanding how women come to be in these types of situations, and how we can undertake to develop a more empathetic, non-judgemental approach to working with them and their families. It is important in our work to remember that each and every member of our society has a story, a past and a circumstance or set of circumstances that have paved the way to where they are in their lives when their path crosses yours. This needs to be considered and respected, and must become an important factor in your approach to intervention with families. The lives and well-being of our society and of the people and families we serve depend on it.

Section Three:

Experiencing Change:
Making a Difference

Chapter 10

Reflections on My Journey and Social Work Education

Tionda Cain

Introduction: Why I Choose Social Work

Like many social workers, challenging life experiences combined with my commitment to social justice led me to choose social work as a career. Being born into a Black, single-parent, low-income family exposed me to some of the harsh realities of racism, poverty and single parenthood. I grew up in a government housing project in a community of marginalized and forgotten people in Toronto. In addition to poverty, many people in my neighbourhood struggled with issues related to mental illness, addictions, family violence, disability, aging, and immigration. From a very young age I was very painfully aware of the range and complexity of a number of social issues. I couldn't accept that "this was just the way it was" for some people and that people who were living under these circumstances somehow deserved it or caused it.

From a young age I was bombarded with oppressive messages of what and who I should be based on my gender, race, and class.

I was told that I would be pregnant and on social assistance by the time I was eighteen. I was encouraged by a guidance counsellor to go to trade school and take something like hairdressing instead of being encouraged to go to university, even though I clearly expressed an interest in being the first person in my family to go to university. I struggled to define myself, love myself and hang on to my self-worth in unhealthy relationships. It was hard to imagine my full potential, to imagine the possibilities that lay beyond the walls of my housing complex. I was riddled with self-doubt, tempted by despair and struggled with the shame and blame that resulted from internalizing the oppressive messages coming at me from all sides.

With the support of family, friends and yes, a good social worker, I resisted the limitations imposed on me and I am proud to say that I continue to resist and am consciously creating a life for myself that I find meaningful and satisfying. It is because of my background and experience that I am interested in working with other people in their struggle to define and change the social, political, and economic aspects of their lives.

This chapter explores how my journey led me to study social work in Halifax, Nova Scotia, in the context of the largest indigenous Black community in Canada. I will talk about some of my experiences and challenges during my first year of social work school and will discuss some of the ways that race and racism have influenced and shaped my learning.

Connecting With History

Having worked in the human service field for many years, I decided that I wanted to return to university to obtain professional designation in social work, ground my practice in theory, and deepen my analysis of oppression. I decided to relocate to Halifax, Nova Scotia, to reconnect with my family roots, learn more about my Black Canadian history and heritage and study social work within this context. I was craving Black professional role models and support. After not having much support through my first degree and few Black role models, I was excited to hear about Black organizations and services such as the Association of Black Social Workers, the Black Educators Association and the Black Student Advising Centre that existed specifically to service the needs of Black individuals, families, and communities.

I had also heard that the Director of the School of Social Work at Dalhousie University, Dr. Wanda Thomas Bernard, was a Black woman from one of the historic Black communities in Nova Scotia. I wanted and needed to know this woman. How did she get to where she was? What was it like for her to be working in the white, male-dominated world of academia? What wisdom and/or survival strategies could she offer? I also wanted to know more about the Racism, Violence and Health Project, a national five-year action research project that Dr. Bernard heads that is looking at the effects of the violence of racism on Black Canadians' health and well-being.

I had been immersed in the rhetoric of diversity and multiculturalism for so long and told not to "dwell on race," that "race doesn't matter" and "don't let racism bring you down" so many times in my life that I actually started to believe race was a part of my identity that I shouldn't focus on. Learning that race and anti-Black racism was openly talked about and acknowledged in Nova Scotia and that people were acknowledging that it did matter, that it did impact your life and your world view, broke a sense of isolation and invisibility that I had been feeling for most of my life.

Growing up in Toronto I was often told that I was "whitewashed." Being of Black Canadian descent didn't meet the criteria for true "blackness" by some of my of Black Caribbean, Black African and African American peers. At the time I had no retort for this accusation, this insult. I didn't have much contact with my family in Nova Scotia. I learned nothing about Black Canadian history in school. I tried my hardest to be successful and to fit into the predominately white society I was born into. I was determined not to live on the margins for the rest of my life. All this left me feeling like I had no history, no heritage, and no distinct culture to be proud of. In addition, I was starting to believe that there wasn't really a place for me in this world because I didn't see any images that even remotely resembled me, my family or my life circumstances in professional settings, the education system, politics or even on TV. I was indeed being washed over by whiteness.

When I decided to study social work in Nova Scotia I was coming back to my roots, to connect with my people, my history. I have discovered that I do have a fascinating history and heritage that I am proud of. I have found the role models and support that I have been looking for. I haven't been granted honorary membership in the Black communities here nor have I found the profound sense of belonging that I had hoped for.

In fact, I initially felt an increased sense of isolation as I slowly discovered profound differences in my experience and the Black Nova Scotian experience. For example, I have had Black Nova Scotians express perplexity and disapproval over my comfort and closeness with white people and my white friends. Experiences of blatant racism and segregation have taught many Black Nova Scotians to be wary of white folks. I know people who went to school in a segregated system here in Nova Scotia and were taunted, teased, assaulted, and called nigger by white people. The racism that I experienced growing up was largely systemic and something I couldn't name until later on in life. The white kids who lived in my neighbourhood and went to school with me in Toronto became my friends and allies rather than my tormentors and enemies. Learning the history of survival, resistance and oppression of Blacks in Nova Scotia will be essential to me being able to practise social work in the Black communities here. Being Black alone will not be enough. I will also need to spend time in communities, with people, investing in relationships.

Theorizing Race in the Classroom

It has been liberating to deepen my analysis around some of the root causes of my oppression and to become more aware of how political, social and economic structures work to oppress and marginalize certain groups. It has been liberating to theorize about oppression, to uncover its tactics and its many faces and to see how people resist it and work to change their social realities. However, this process of consciousness raising has also been painful, uncomfortable and emotional. It is hard to discuss issues in the classroom that hit so close to home, that are so deeply personal, that have caused so much pain. Often times I have sat through many class discussions choked silent by emotion. Being in social work school is like doing an in-depth case study analysis on my life and those who are closest to me.

The social work school that I attend teaches social work from an anti-oppressive philosophy and perspective. This means that an analysis of power and structural inequalities on people's lives are incorporated into the curriculum and there is a focus on social action and social change. We frequently talk about the ways people experience oppression based on gender, race, class, ability, age, sexual orientation and so on. It is so important to have an analysis in order to avoid attributing the present state of inequality to individual or racial inadequacies.

It has been particularly difficult for me to talk about race in the classroom, especially in a classroom full of white students. Inevitably the discussion always ends up focusing on the topic of white privilege. White students are either racked with guilt over it, minimize it, are blissfully unaware of the benefits that they derive from it, or are proud to exclaim that they are aware of their white privilege and their racism. Ironically, it is white privilege itself that feeds the sense of entitlement that white people feel takes up so much space in a conversation about racism. Their privilege continues to centre their experience in these discussions and marginalize other experiences. The discussion is usually further fuelled by anger among students of colour when people minimize and deny white privilege and racism. I was once in a three-hour anti-racism workshop where the majority of the workshop focused on comforting, consoling and counselling one white participant who was racked with guilt over her privilege and was very disturbed that the term "racist" was being used in any other context outside of referring to Hitler.

Even if these discussions could be facilitated in a more constructive balanced way, it probably wouldn't make it any easier for me to engage in these conversations because I have little interest in talking about white privilege with white people. It has taken me a long time to get over the guilt that I have over my lack of patience for the discussions described above. I do recognize that these conversations are important to have, that they can create understanding across difference. However, I am tired of offering up the pain I have experienced from racism (and the denial of racism) for cross-cultural educational purposes. More and more I am seeing the necessity of white people taking on some of the challenge of educating other white people about racism.

I am more interested in talking about the strategies people of colour are employing to resist the negative impacts of racism in their lives, about how they are getting by without white privilege. I want to talk about how things like gender, class, age and sexual orientation impact a person's experience of racism. I want to talk about what it means to heal from racism's devastating effects while still constantly being bombarded with racism on a daily basis. I want to hear about what Black people are doing to uncover and confront their internalized oppression. I want to open a dialogue about the fear, distrust and disgust that Black people have of each other and how this is impacting our capacity to be mutually supportive and collectively effective. But these are difficult conversations to have in a room full of white people. How can we even start to talk about creating allies across race when people are having difficulty creating alliances within their racial group?

In the emotional uproar and focus on white privilege, a discussion about how the different ways in which we all possess privilege in some form is lost. The discussion is then limited by the dichotomy of "those who have and those who have not," those who are oppressed and those who are not. Alternately, I have witnessed some explosive interactions where people have aggressively minimized someone's experience of racism by pointing to the ways in which they oppress others. I am reminded of a time in a class where we were sharing our different experiences of oppression, a white male student tried to explain how many of us are guilty of buying coffee at Tim Hortons and this was an exercise of privilege and how this act was supporting the economic oppression of campesino coffee farmers in Central/South America. A number of low-income students of colour responded angrily to his comment because they felt their own experience of oppression was being dismissed or ranked less important. These conversations are always messy and people often leave feeling hurt, shutdown, and/or angry.

Centring Black Experience in the Classroom

I had the opportunity to take the only Africentric Perspectives in Social Work course offered in Canada. It was such a relief to be in a class where the professor looked like me, the majority of the class were people of colour, and the entire class content (not just one week) was directly related to me and had significance and relevance in my life. I have often found that I am usually one of maybe two or three people of colour in a classroom full of white students. When this happens over and over again I can't help but wonder, "Am I supposed to be here?" The messages that I received from my guidance counsellor still linger in my head. Sometimes it is the internalized racism rather than externalized racism and barriers that are the biggest obstacles to Black students excelling in school.

There are many internal processes that I struggle with when I walk into a classroom full of white students in order for me to adapt, protect myself, and be on guard for racism. I wonder if people will talk to me; I worry that I will be put on the spot and asked to speak on behalf of the entire Black race. I worry that I will feel obligated to defend the entire Black race, or give personal life examples of painful experiences of individual/systemic racism for educational purposes. I worry about being articulate but more than anything, I worry that even if I find the courage to speak up in a classroom of all-white students my contribution will be met with blank white stares and an uncomfortable silence. It was wonderful to have the experience where my contributions to the class discussion were not only acknowledged but also validated and echoed by other people's experiences (including the professor's).

I came into my Africentric Perspectives in Social Work class questioning whether or not it is realistic to try and attempt to have an Africentric theory or framework for understanding Black African peoples' experience when we are so diverse and so dispersed throughout the Diaspora. Is there a common African world view? Is there a common experience? Is there a common solution to the plight of Black African people in the world? My professor says that the experience that all people of African descent share is racism. But is the shared experience of racism enough to unite us? And what about sexism, classism, heterosexism, ableism and all of the other faces of oppressions? Will these issues that also deeply impact lives get lost or be overrided by race issues?

Like Jerome Schiele (1994), I am critical of a monolithic view of African culture. I am skeptical of a theory that claims to capture the ethos of African values when Africa and her descendants are so diverse and values and culture change over time. However, through this course I was able to recognize that Africentricity does more than promote African values; it offers a more humane alternative to the Eurocentric world view that encourages social equality, social justice and social transformation (Schiele, 1994).

Inevitably, a Eurocentric world view that values and places emphasis on individualism, material wealth, and competition can only result in isolation, greed, hierarchy and many people "losing" (Schiele, 1994). It is one thing to work to change oppressive systems/structures but it is quite another thing to change the dominant world view. The challenge feels overwhelming and in many ways seems impossible. My own unlearning of Eurocentric values and ways of being has been a significant challenge and requires me to regularly check taken-for-granted assumptions and attitudes, and the way I relate to others. If we truly want to change the world we have to change the way we see it and that change has to begin on a personal level. As Schiele (1994) says, Africentricity offers an alternative world view, one based on principles of collectivity, inter-connectedness, spirituality and the valuing of affective knowledge.

It has been said that interconnection is the cornerstone of Afri-centric theory. A sense of interconnection is so important to facili-tate the development of social relationships, collective identity, and get people looking out for one another. But I see this principle as probably one of the most difficult or challenging for Black people to live out in our racist society. I have seen how racism assaults Black people and can make some very angry, suspicious, and bitter. It is difficult to connect with others across such powerful and nega-tive emotions.

As a social worker, I am interested in facilitating a process where Black folks can work through these emotions, begin to heal, and begin to connect again with the world in more intimate and healthy ways. I keep wondering, how do we do this? Where do we start? Then I am reminded of my experience in the talking circles at the 2003 Black Community Forum put on by the Racism, Vio-lence and Health Project. We must begin by centring Black peo-ple's experience and by acknowledging affective knowledge and the spiritual aspect of our being. We must begin by talking to each other.

I went into this course focused more on the differences rather than similarities of African people throughout the Diaspora. I am leaving this course still with an awareness and appreciation for our diversity but also with a deeper awareness of how our shared strug-gles and history unite us on a spiritual and political level.

The Illusion of Diversity

It is hard not to think about race and racism in a place like Nova Scotia, which has the largest indigenous Black population in Canada, where the racial divides are physically apparent, where only a small percentage of Black students actually graduate from high school and Africville reunions act as consistent reminders of the horrific treatment of Black people in this province. African Nova Scotian communities have responded to anti-Black racism with resilience, creativity, solidarity and strength. However, in the rhetoric of "celebrating diversity" it has become more and more difficult to point out and address racism in Nova Scotia.

I went to a conference last month where I quickly became aware of the fact that I was likely the only Black person in the auditorium. Hmmm, I said to myself. Do I ignore this piece of information and just focus on the keynote address? I scanned the room to see if there might at least be another who was visibly a person of colour. Nope, not that I could see. At this point I was feeling very Black, very uncomfortable, and very angry. Why is it that in a relatively diverse city such as Halifax, at a conference talking about inspiring healing conversations with individuals, families and communities, there are no Black people?

Just as I was thinking that I am tired of being the only Black person or person of colour in spaces that are created to talk about healing, social change, and activism, I run into a Black woman. We look at each other with surprise and then delight. She gives me *two* big hugs and tells me it is so good to see another Black person and how she too was feeling frustrated, disappointed, and discouraged with the lack of diversity in the crowd. I find comfort, understanding and relief in her embrace. It was so empowering and affirming to have my thoughts and feelings validated by this woman.

Sometimes I feel invisible or hypersensitive in those situations. It worries me that no one even mentions the obvious anymore, let alone questions what might be wrong with an all-white picture. It makes me furious to raise the point only to have people respond by asking me to "recruit" other people of colour or give suggestions for "attracting" a more diverse crowd. Others will express confusion over why more people of colour didn't come even though it was so well advertised in Aboriginal and Black communities but not give another thought to it since they did make the effort after all and it is totally understandable if those people choose to self-segregate. I can see and have experienced the value in working with allies across difference, across oppressions, and seeing the interconnectedness of our struggles. But building those alliances within and across differences can be frustrating, isolating and discouraging.

Conclusion

With my budding consciousness came an increased desire to collectively work for social change within a community of Black people who share similar concerns, issues and experiences, hoping that this would break the sense of isolation and invisibility and would strengthen and encourage the efficacy of my social analysis and action. My desire has led me to understand how this will not be as easy as I thought it would be and that I also wanted to create and be part of a diverse community of people who are committed to social change.

As I go into my second year of social work school I am thinking a lot about working across race, working with difference, and building relationships both inside and outside the Black communities. Even though my childhood struggles don't seem that far away from me, I am reminded that the combination of my education, international experience, and my unique experience of growing up in Toronto has created differences between me, my family, the people I love and grew up with, and the people I hope to work with one day here in Nova Scotia. I want to be attentive to issues of power and my assumptions that arise out of my notions of sameness and difference. I want to more consciously make the connections between local and global struggles and continue to try to build a community based on shared hopes and a shared vision of social justice.

References

Schiele, J. (1994). Afrocentricity as an alternative world view for equality. *Journal of Progressive Human Services*, 5(1), 5-52.

Chapter 11

Reconnection:
Finding Identity and Truth
"A Journey Within"

Darlamaine Gero-Hagel

One can go through life and simply participate according to the rules and norms of the dominant society, never knowing or understanding who one truly is nor one's purpose in life. For half a century it seems I have been going through the motions of life, searching for an unknown but not knowing what that unknown was. This is a powerfully sad yet therapeutic healing endeavour for me.

According to Martin and Martin (2005), my life experience and circumstance is synonymous with a bibliotherapy, "historical empathy." Martin and Martin state that reading about the lives and struggles of Black people through historical narratives, biographies and autobiographies can strengthen ancestral empathy and connectedness (p. 254). This bibliotherapy has been the building block of my identity. I feel I have suffered a devastating disconnection from the African community of which I am a part but was not allowed to participate in for several reasons. I will elaborate on this point later on.

I see, feel, sense, and am drawn to the reconnection of my African ancestors. I say reconnect because I feel I have endured a heartbreaking disconnect as a child. Forever on a quest to fit pieces of an historical life puzzle together, I have never understood why I was different, and never "fit" into the "white world." I have a very clear, albeit bittersweet, picture now which will become clear by the end of my story. This chapter will be divided into various significant parts: my journey, my autobiography, white privilege, Africentricity, my learning/growth and conclusion.

The Journey

On this journey, my analogy, I sense always feeling that I have been stumbling along a winding mountainous path with unsure footing, lacking direction and destiny. Curves and crevasses, blurred vision, obstacles to navigate, always on the edge of the abyss which may lie around the next bend. Given my experiences I felt I was on the brink of passing over or falling into the abyss on more than one occasion. Fear, racism discrimination and intersecting levels of oppression were a constant in my life; I did not fully comprehend the impact of the internalization of the oppression, living day to day within society imbued with oppression in all systems. I do not want this journey to be one of doom and gloom, as it is not; it is reality, my life. However, there are elements and circumstances that give this inference. I have never been one to wallow in self-pity, as time and strength never allowed me to be this type of individual.

I now understand resilience and just how resilient I have become. Protective factors, critical elements in the development of resilience, fall into three categories: individual characteristics, supportive family and positive relationship with at least one parent or relative, and available and useful external community supports.

I believe I did possess these elements, some greater than others, which kept me grounded for the most part throughout my life. My sister and I are very healthy in all spheres but my brothers did not fare as well; one is institutionalized and the other battles addiction problems.

I know my tone may seem depersonalized at times, but in my quest for the truth, it seems I was standing outside myself looking backwards, inwards, sideways, forwards – always reflecting, deconstructing, rebuilding, critically analyzing, and at times turning myself inside out looking for me and who I really was and am today. Therefore, it seems at times I am speaking of an individual outside of myself. Not knowing or understanding my African culture and how integral and critical to my sense of self and identity it is, I have been seeking what the meanings in my life are and were, why tragic events happened as they did. Where did I come from, what was I, who was I, where did I "fit" into this world? At times and different developmental life stages the world was a very painful and unforgiving place for a Black child, girl, daughter, woman, mother, grandmother, sister and aunt. So many questions and so few answers.

This journey is the search for my identity, my people and culture and an opportunity to now challenge my fears, know my history and find out who I really am: in short, my quest for truth. This has been presented to me as a gift, an outstretched hand inviting me to embark upon the adventure in order to find out who and what I have been searching for. For this I am deeply grateful.

Autobiography

I am the oldest daughter of four children of Fredric Mclellan Gero and Joan Marjorie Gero. I have an older brother, Daryl, a younger brother, Duane, who was adopted and is of Jamaican origin, and my sister Laurie is the youngest. My father is African Nova Scotian, originally from the New Glasgow area. My mother was white, of Scottish heritage. Her family disowned her when she married outside her race, and it was not until Daryl was born that my grandmother grudgingly began to accept race mixing.

My parents divorced eighteen years later, due to continual conflict and my mother's infidelity, which was an ongoing problem in the marriage.

Given my father was in the military, we often relocated from base to base within Canada. My parents came west to Edmonton, Alberta, when Daryl and I were very young. I know my father had postings in between, at which times we would stay in Kingston, or travel by train from Edmonton back home. The train porters were always an exciting part of the trip for me as I used to sit for long periods chattering away to them. They would give me candy but only with permission from my mother. I never could understand why they had to ask my mother; candy was candy to this little girl. I remember vividly the porters' red hats and uniforms and for some reason I felt at peace or a sense of comfort and belonging being with them. I now think I was missing my father as he was absent for long periods of time, off to unknown far away places, and I subsequently identified with these Black men. After all, they did look like my daddy, uncles, cousins and all the relatives in my father's family. We took the train to Kingston often, as whenever my father took a long posting, military policy was to send the family back to my mother's hometown.

I know moving to Edmonton was very hard for my parents, and the racism was so overt. My parents tried renting a home off the base. When my mother went she would secure the place, but as soon as the landlord saw my father, Daryl and I the place mistakenly had been rented. My mother would be infuriated that they would rent to a white woman, but not to a Black family. This forced my parents to buy a home on "civvy street" where we became known as the "niggers on the block" and my mother was called a "nigger lover."

Edmonton was painful for all of us, as Daryl and I began school there. Not only were the adults and kids cruel, so were the institutions. I was IQ tested and labeled "retarded," and put into a "special class." Not understanding, I thought I was special. I was special alright! I think now some of my learning difficulties were attributed to the fact that I was left-handed and I was forcibly switched, as being left-handed in those days was unacceptable. My parents were also informed that I was dyslexic. We were sent home from school to tell our mother to wash us, as we were dirty. This was most frustrating and hurtful, as my mother was a fastidious woman, getting us up early to bathe, and spend what seemed to be hours doing my Black ringlets to perfection, then securing them with pretty bows. She groomed my brother, putting Brylcreme in his hair. Again outraged, my mother confronted the school and told them in no uncertain terms that we were not dirty, we were mulatto children and that was our colour. The irony and truth was we were not allowed to get dirty, ever.

Play was limited because it could not interfere with dance lessons, as my mother feared me falling and skinning my knees – scabs had to be covered with makeup for stage performances. She was obsessed with my lessons. I was in tap, jazz, ballet, Spanish, Highland, and ballroom, constantly in competitions and performances. I would be chastised if I received the silver medal and not the gold, as I could always have done better in her eyes. I had to explain to her what I had done wrong that had cost me the gold medal. Silver or second place was never good enough. While I presume most kids were doing homework or playing, I had to practise dance daily. Education was not a priority for my mother. Dance was to be my career; therefore, there was little emphasis put on schooling, although we attended regularly. I had the best of the best as far as clothing, with all of the beautiful costumes, dancing shoes, outfits, and dresses. I now think my mother was living her dreams through me, as she longed to be a professional dancer.

Given the standards of the day, I guess we would have been deemed lower middle class. I would often invite poor white girls home and take out all of my sequined costumes and dresses, letting them try them on, trying to give away things under my mother's watchful eye. She asked me once, "Why do you always have to bring home all the ragamuffins, sickly animals with one eye glued shut, runts, and bloody lame dogs?" I could not answer her as I did not know what she meant. I did not know myself why. It seems I was always trying to spare people and animals some of the pain

I was enduring. All I knew was I always felt sorry for them and wanted to give them things or help them. I had so much in comparison, as my father was a good provider, and I guess the military was the place to be.

I would watch my father polish his brass continually, and spit polish his boots. His uniforms were impeccable; he used to jokingly say, "Be careful – you will cut your fingers on the creases of those shirts and pants." He was the one who taught me to iron, and I used to love pressing and starching his army shirts to perfection. He was one proud, handsome soldier. He could sing like Nat King Cole, as well as play every instrument you could think of and he still does to this day. He is a very gifted musician. When I was very ill, with childhood migraine headaches and sick with scarlet fever, he would sit on my bed and sing to me. I was so close to my father, often faking illness so he would not go away. It didn't work.

I used to cry about the name calling and the jingles as I never knew what a "nigger" was but learned very quickly. And what I grew up with.

My father drummed into my head, "You have to work harder than everyone else, you have to be cleaner than everyone else, you have to dress better than everyone else, you have to be smarter than everyone else, you have to be stronger than everyone else, and you have to be kinder than everyone else, just to get along." And "Be proud of who you are." I don't think I ever really understood the strong meaning and lessons behind his words until I was much older. It was hard to be proud when I got my front teeth knocked out in the schoolyard, saw my brother fighting, all while being called nigger, over and over. I grew to hate the word, once I understood what it meant and the torment and pain it caused us all. My brother always fought; conversely, I would run away as fast as I could, crying, running to the safe confines of home, at least safer than the schoolyard.

On one of our excursions home to Kingston, we ended up staying for three long anguishing years while my father went to Indo China. My mother became more obsessive, physically, emotionally and mentally abusive with more frequency. On one occasion I could not go to school for a week as I was black and blue with bruises from her angry fists and feet. By this time Duane had been adopted and was home with us. We had him since birth so it was no big deal to us kids. It was also at this time my mother had an ongoing affair with a mutual friend of my parents. I had the misfortune and shock of finding the two together, which really broke my heart. I angrily told her I was going to tell my father but this only served to get me more beatings and the mental and emotional abuse escalated for both me and my oldest brother.

I think I was targeted more as I ached, cried, and pined away for my father, which really aggravated my mother. I verbalized this to her as well, often stealing her hidden letters from him and reading as much as I could. This white man, the mutual friend whom I grew to despise, is my sister's father. This does not detract from the wonderful relationship and love that I have for her and the family.

My father returned home knowing about the pregnancy and we returned to Edmonton, hiding this secret for a while. My father fully accepted this man's child as his own. My sister has no Black blood; she has blonde hair and blue eyes, which was all I ever wanted to be, and I tried to be using Ajax, and bleach in the bath. I always knew the girls with white skin and blue or green eyes had a good life and were never teased.

I had begun to dislike my mother for many reasons. Her abuse towards us children and my father escalated mentally, physically, and emotionally. She became more angry, obsessive and controlling. I grieved on many fronts, and was severely traumatized by her failing to protect me from her pedophile brother. The lying, cheating, threats and broken promises impacted me tremendously. I resented her robbing me of my African culture and forcing us to assimilate and conform to her family ways.

There is an abundance of family history and stories that is beyond the scope of this chapter. Nevertheless, I have tried to capture significant albeit tragic life events and losses.

I have suffered many losses throughout my life thus far, which have become what I call "scars upon the heart." The loss of innocence at a tender age due to sexual assault, incest and going to trial was difficult to work through. The loss of my family on both sides and the fracturing effects of my parents' divorce were excruciating. The loss of my mother when she was so young and the devastating effects of her suicide that traumatized all us children still leave their mark. Further, the loss of teenage years, freedom, education, and the struggle to keep a shattered family together, as I quit school to parent my siblings and go to work, served to build strength and character.

Confused as to what love was and feeling unworthy I sought love out in detrimental ways. This lent itself to drug abuse, promiscuity, abusive toxic relationships albeit brief, sad but true, accompanied by the pain and shame that is associated with destructive behaviour. I must also say, I was a teen when I was introduced to drugs by my daughter's father, a white married man ten years my senior. Also, I had lost self-esteem, self-worth, innocence, family, culture and identity in childhood so I never could find myself. I too had individuals who preyed upon my gullibility, naïveté and pain, and exploited me in criminal ways.

To be abundantly clear, I have never been charged with a crime, sold a drug, harmed a child, nor anyone throughout life, as I was self-absorbed in hurting myself with the help and knowledge of older white males, one being my police officer boyfriend. Further, fortunately I have never been involved with any of the formal systems. I lost trust in adults when I was a child, which has taken me years to rebuild. The turning point in my life was the birth of my daughter when I was twenty, as I vowed never to use another drug, and commenced a path of healing. I feel the primary supports that I had in life were on my father's side of the family, save for one uncle on my mother's side who I saw occasionally.

White Privilege

Given the Eurocentric side of my mother's family I do not know if my mother really comprehended her white privilege or thought through to any extent the effects of marrying outside her race and the pain it would bring.

According to Peggy MacIntosh (1989), the types of privilege my mother would be afforded are the following: The freedom to associate exclusively or primarily with members of your own group. The level of social acceptance one can presume across varying contexts. The ability to see members of your groups in a positive light, in the records of history, in texts, in media, and as role models. The freedom from stereotyping. The ability to be oblivious of other groups. The ability to feel at home in the world. (p. 155).

I believe she received support from her family, but this was not extended to us children. However, my sister does maintain a relationship with members of our mother's side of the family. My brothers and I do not nor do I wish to.

This stated, my mother must have also had to play multiple roles in life, but still had the option to be freed of some of the racism and oppression if she chose. The point is, she always had choice. I know she too suffered intersecting levels of oppression: the military wife, her gender, the times, the wife and mother of an African man with African children, with the exception of my sister who enjoys "white" privilege and does not understand any differences within our family members. Even knowing really we are half sisters and her biological father is a white man whom she has never met is her choice. All said, she is never questioned about her "whiteness" or culture as it is not visible.

I believe the context of the times, the social and political fabric of society, still ascribes to white female privilege based upon Black female history – the colonization, slavery and emancipation of Black women, as we remain inferior to white women. White women have benefited and continue to reap rewards on the backs of Black women. So I do not believe we are equal and enjoying the same freedoms. Without freedom, how can equality and social justice come to fruition? I believe there is a necessity to challenge female white privilege, by non-white women in order to facilitate change within dominant institutions, systems, families and structures.

As Ruth Frankenberg writes (1997): "Attention to the construction of White 'experience' is important, both to transforming the meaning of Whiteness and to transforming the relations of race in general. This is crucial in a social context in which the racial order is normalized and rationalized rather than upheld by coercion alone. Analyzing the connections between White daily lives and discursive orders may help make visible the processes by which the stability of Whiteness – as location of privilege, as culturally normative space, and as standpoint – is secured and reproduced. In this context, reconceptualizing histories and refiguring racialized landscapes are political acts in themselves" (p. 80).

I find these to be accurate and profound statements made by Black women from the African Diaspora, with the necessity to boldly challenge the social order. The challenge must be proactive and sustained in order to have consequence on the status quo.

I know life was a challenge for both my parents, and they too faced horrific racism. I squarely place the blame upon my parents for disallowing the nurturing of the African side of my family, more so my mother than my father. I do believe my father tried to maintain the culture but was overridden by my overbearing mother, and I also believe, given the times, it was probably easier for my father to conform than to carry on the fight. I am cognizant of the fact that the military authoritarian hierarchy was indeed a contributing factor to my father conforming to the mainstream to the extent he was permitted. The military assimilated my father as much as possible, as did the Eurocentric side of the family unit. In addition, this runs contrary to Africentric perspectives. I can see this as a serious clash of world views, values, morals, roles, expectations, institutions and such, between two very different cultures and the composition of the family. It is undeniable and inevitable that this would be a critical source of conflict between the cultures.

According to Robert Hill (1998), "Although Africans recognize the mother-child dyad as a primary social and affective unit . . . it is erroneous to characterize this unit as a separate 'nuclear family' within the African extended family. Such a formulation has no explanatory value since none of the normal functions of a family were traditionally performed by this unit in isolation. It was not a unit of socialization in and of itself; it was not a unit of economic production or consumption in and of itself; it was not an isolated unit of emotional support or mutual aid; it obviously was not a procreative unit. Why then term it 'nuclear family?'" (pp. 11, 15).

According to Hatchett and Holmes (1999), there are five ways or modes of adapting in adjustment to the social structure: (1) conformity, (2) innovation, (3) retreatism, (4) ritualism, (5) rebellion (p. 72).

In addition, I witnessed retreatism in my father, which was forced upon him and was perhaps a saving grace for him. Often I see sadness in my father and I believe external and internal racism did take their toll on him throughout the years and stole some of his spirit. When I spoke with him for this chapter he stated, "I miss home now and then. I never thought about home much after I left but I did enjoy my trip home in 1995." I sensed or felt an underlying sorrow within him. Both he and my aunt speak of Africville, describing what it was like when they were young, as they remember it well.

My mother disapproved of the Baptist church so we were removed, and indoctrinated into her Presbyterian church. As my father said, "Your mother got tired of the moaning, groaning, wailing and craziness of the Baptist church as she saw it." When we went to Nova Scotia and Montreal to visit my father's family she was absent. These were joyous visits; I remember fondly so many relatives, cousins to play with, abundance of different foods, church, singing Black gospel music and hymns, laughter, warmth, love — in sum, a whole lot of fun. I never felt more at home and a sense of belonging than when these joyful visits happened, and I never wanted to leave. Unfortunately, they were few and far between.

I guess it was the collective and community of my African family that seemed to resonate within me. I fostered a long and loving relationship with my Nan Gero, aunties and uncles. The loss of my Nan in 1990 was a monumental loss for me. However, over time and few visits so much of the culture was lost. My aunt Margarite remains a very prominent person in my life and a link to my past.

I think it was just easier for my father to give in to my mother's demands rather than battle with her, as he is a passive, loving, caring man who sent money home to his family much to my mother's chagrin. This too was a source of conflict for them. In time I grew to loathe my mother for all the things she had done and not done for us. I feel the following quotation speaks to my inner feelings as an unprepared child growing up in a racist society. As Banks-Wallace and Parks (2001) state, "Mother-daughter relationships are one of many human experiences significantly influenced by race and racism" (p. 96).

My mother's attitude was "get used to it. What is wrong with you? Do you need your head read?" and on and on. It was the sexual assault that was to be the severing of my relationship with my mother and her family and the cause of the alienation that ensued. The shame that was brought to the family upon a five-year-old girl's disclosure left me on the outside looking in, just as my pedophile uncle guaranteed it would. He was never charged, but my mother assured me he would never be permitted in our home again. Another lie.

From that day forward I was never to be part of the family; I was simply present in body, hating every minute of it. Everyone knew of the assault but somehow the uncle was forgiven, a bitter pill for me to swallow. A classic example of "blaming the victim" mentality, which I assume was the norm in my mother's family. It was most difficult to comprehend this concept as a child of five years. The only happy memories I have of Kingston are the times going to the cottage at the lake, swimming, boating and fishing, hence my fondness for lakes and oceans. Perhaps this contributes to my longing for Nova Scotia, where it all began so long ago.

African Culture and Africentricity

I feel much of my confusion in life is a result of being stranded between two cultures, with some understanding of my African culture, which was not permitted to be nurtured and kept alive. I understand this culture and many of the principles; this is basically how I live my life in many respects: the collectivity, the holistic approach to life, and the spirituality. I am now connected to Africentricity after being disconnected for so long; I am centred. Being caught in the "crossfire" of two polarized cultures has been my burden to bear and at times I have felt most despairing. According to Jerome Schiele (1994), "central to the nature of the cosmological and the axiological attributes of the Afrocentric world view is the emphasis on interdependency, collectivity, and spirituality" (p. 15).

When I was with my father's family this overtly rang true and I must have absorbed a great deal at the time. I believe that my African culture was not permitted by my mother or mainstream society. My mother was forcing us to "fit" into her white culture, probably knowing this was impossible. Perhaps her struggles and years of oppression were her demise. I know she was severely sexually abused as a child by her father, which may have also desensitized her about this subject and fostered the anger within her. In addition, I appreciate she had a hard life and suffered from mental illness.

I worked through my inner anger and pain and forgave my mother long ago. I needed to do this for my mental and emotional well-being. I believe we had a "love/hate" relationship. The good qualities she instilled in us unfortunately were outweighed by the bad. We were different; we were Black children suffering in her world, primarily with forced Eurocentric norms and values of the dominant group. Because our dad was gone so often it was easy to eliminate the African culture.

Frances Welshing (1991) points out that Eurocentric culture is "a system into which non-white people never can be integrated" (p. 255). Prophetic words, the reality past and present. I used to believe my dad being absent was his defense mechanism, a form of escapism from my mother's wrath and I still believe this to be true. I do not fault him for this – I understand. Granted, we have had our issues to work through over the years, and have done so. We do enjoy a healthy happy relationship now, and have for several years.

Identity and Growth

Now I can look back on my life to date, and understand and put things into perspective. I went through my unhealthy years before my daughter was born and did change my life. I healed and moved on, leaving the garbage in the dump. After the abusive alcoholic years with my sons' father I chose a new path when they were very young, giving way to single parenthood. I went to nursing school and obtained my diploma, as I never wanted the stigma attached to us being "welfare labeled" and unfortunately there is great stigma attached to the system. I had gone through life with enough labels, stereotyping, oppression, racism, pain and suffering and wanted a different life for myself and my children.

I always knew the key was higher education and I also wanted to be a positive role model for my children. This has happened and I have happy, healthy, educated children who are a source of pride for me; two are married and have their own children. My youngest son remains home and is pursuing a career in law enforcement. Further, I now have many roles to fulfill besides daughter, sister, auntie, mother, wife, friend and Nana. I have an obligation to continue the African culture within my family and do so with pride.

I believe I entered the nursing profession as I saw it as a helping discipline, and I think this concept was present in my childhood. I had empathy, compassion and the ability to sympathize with those that were in pain – physical, emotional, mental or otherwise. As I healed throughout my life, I believe I had the passion to extend and offer the gifts I had been given to others that were and are suffering. However, the cutbacks in nursing and the erosion of the healthcare social safety net, the work load and unsafe conditions became unbearable. Further, twenty years of physical lifting, shift work, and overall demands took their toll on me physically, leaving me riddled with arthritis. With my spouse's support, I returned to college.

Social work seemed like a natural fit, and fostered my commitment and passion to the helping profession. My desire for social justice and my zealous quest to eradicate racism fans the flames of my desire to achieve and to challenge these issues that permeate society. Interestingly, I am employed as a social worker in a government patriarchal system imbued with oppression. From obtaining my diploma in social work, I went on to the University of Alberta, majoring in native studies, minoring in anthropology. Obtaining my BA in 1999, I then continued on to the University of Calgary, completing my BSW in 2002. I am currently in the Master of Social Work program at Dalhousie University, an important part of my learning journey to gain more skills and power to confront and challenge ongoing oppression and social injustice within society. I too wish to honour my father, my African ancestors and family as well, for their historical years of oppression, and the horrific racism they endured.

Conclusion

Writing this chapter has offered me the opportunity to delve into my past, look at history and to search for who I am. I knew I wanted to embark on this journey hoping to find answers, gain knowledge, to learn and grow. There were times completing this journey that were very emotional and powerful for me. I have achieved my goal and the personal growth is tremendous.

I can now definitively say I am a proud African woman, with a rich history and culture. I may have been robbed of this for a large portion of my life, but I can now live knowing who I am and where I came from with immense pride. I too can become involved with the African community as this is also where my personal truth lies. It is where I belong, where I can recapture and reconnect with the acceptance of my collective African community. The truth and my identity never left me; they were there inside all along amidst the toxicity. Unfortunately, I ingested an abundance of "poison" throughout developmental life stages and experiences. However, I can now foster my self-worth, self-esteem and confidence, working at ridding myself of old demons that I internalized which destroyed my true identity. My journey has now come to an end in one sense, but another journey awaits as I can now find inner peace and move towards further growth and healing. I now understand the inner longing, the pull towards Nova Scotia, my father's and ancestors' home.

I asked my father yesterday, "Dad, how do you see me, what race am I?" He responded, "If you have any Black blood at all then that is what you are; you are considered Black." I believe I now have found truth from the African man, my father, my African Nova Scotian family and my ancestors. Incredibly, throughout my life I never asked this simple question. Perhaps fear of the journey held me back. Finding truth, seizing my identity, reconnecting and deconstructing, being allowed to be who and what I am. I may technically be biracial, but I belong to one race, the African race. This has been an incredible journey. The mountainous path is now clear and I can see what's ahead. I have a vision. I can now live without fear and have a sense of my destiny. How liberating for this African woman's spirit, for a woman who has lived with a deadened spirit for far too long. My passion for combating racism and the ongoing battle for social justice will be much more vigorous, as I continue life's journey, unsure of where it will take me.

I found this excerpt from the Bradwin Address by Rubin "Hurricane" Carter most enlightening, resonating within me perhaps because it articulated the feeling of being freed from my personal prison:

> You see, there are prisons and there are prisons.
> They may look different, but they're all the same.
> They all confine you. They all limit your free-
> dom. They all lock you away and grind you down

and take a heavy toll on your self-esteem. There are prisons made of steel, brick, and mortar. And then there are prisons without visible walls: the prisons of poverty, illiteracy, and racism. All too often people condemned to these metaphorical prisons (poverty, racism, and illiteracy) end up doing double time; that is, they wind up in the physical prisons as well. Our task is to recognize the interconnectedness and the sameness of all of these prisons.

References

Banks-Wallace, J. & Parks, L. (2001). "So that our souls don't get damaged": the impact of racism on maternal thinking and practice related to the protection of daughters. *Issues in Mental Health Nursing, 22*, 77-98.

Carter, Rubin "Hurricane." Bradwin Address abbreviated version (pp. 34-37). 1993. www.frontiercollege.ca/english/archive/public/newslet/whatnew/feb00/2000.pdf Retrieved August 2005.

Frankenberg, R. (1997). *White women, race matters: The social construction of whiteness.* Durham, N.C. University Press, c. 1997.

Hatchett, B.F. & Holmes, K. (1999). Effects of citizenship inequalities of the Black male challenge. *A Journal of Research on African American Men, 10*(2), 65-77.

Hill, R. (1998). Understanding Black family functioning: A holistic perspective. *Journal of Comparative Family Studies. 29*(1), 27-37.

MacIntosh, P. (1989). "White privilege: Unpacking the invisible knapsack." *Peace and Freedom*, Jul/Aug 1989: 10-12.

Martin, E.P. & Martin, J.M. (1995). *Social work and the Black experience.* Chapter 11, (pp. 250-277). NASW Press.

Schiele, J. (1994). Afrocentricity as an alternative world view for equality. *Journal of Progressive Human Services*, 5(1), 5-52.

Welshing, F.C. (1991). *Racism & Black child and youth inferiorization, The Issis Chapters*. Chicago: Third World Press. (pp. 239-258).

Chapter 12

My Journey So Far

Oluronke Taiwo

I am the second of six siblings. My parents' names are Simeon Olufunmilayo Akindoju and Modupe Florence Akinkugbe, both of whom are indigenes of Ondo, Nigeria, which is also my birthplace. The names given always have a meaning at the time of birth. My name Oluronke signifies that "God has something beautiful to care for" and the prefix "Akin" can be interpreted as a "great warrior," signifying that my ancestors were great warriors, mainly hunters who were worshipers of "Ogun," the god of iron. My great-grandparents later became Christians and this reflected in all our names, which now are preceded by "Oluwa," meaning the "Great God."

Ondo town is located in the western part of Nigeria and it is a Yoruba-speaking ethnic group. The other ethnic groups which speak this common language are Egbado, Ekiti, Oyo, Ile-Ife, Ijesa, and Awori, the different groups of Ijebu, Ilorin and Kabba province (Fadipe, 1970, p. 29; Gordon, 2005). Even though all these towns come from the Yoruba ethnic group, they all speak different dialects, which make the culture unique.

My country, Nigeria, is located on the Western part of Africa, with an estimated population of about 120 million and about 150 to 300 indigenous dialects being spoken. This makes Nigeria the most populous Black nation in the world (*Oduma Magazine*, 1977).

My life has been a journey of beauty, struggle and determination. I started with the word "beauty" because I was brought up in a Christian home that was filled with love and thorough discipline. My parents gave us everything they had: love, joy and discipline. My parents were very strict; growing up, we were taught to respect our elders and to learn good moral values. This upbringing also signifies the norms of our culture. I lost my mother at the early age of twelve. Although the second child of the family, as the first daughter I carried lots of responsibilities at an early age. With younger siblings in the age range of four to ten, I inevitably had to take an active role in their daily care. To ease the responsibility, my father remarried, and he married a wonderful lady who took great care of the six of us as well as her own children. To shoulder such responsibilities at an early age, I have been able to acquire a life of determination and accomplishment right from the beginning.

I was a very bright person growing up. My primary school education was completed at Ideal Primary School and because of my achievements I got a scholarship to attend Saint Anne's School Ibadan (a boarding school for girls) where I successfully completed my secondary school education. With Saint Anne's being a missionary school, discipline was part of our daily routine in addition to learning, and I can boldly say that this has contributed immensely to the success of my journey so far.

Real life's struggles started immediately after my secondary school education. Despite my successful academic accomplishment in secondary school, I was unable to attain the grade I had hoped for and this led me to go into the workforce at an early age of seventeen years. I was able to obtain a job as a laboratory assistant, however, because of my determination; I continue to pursue various laboratory-career related courses on the side. As part of my determination, I enrolled in various courses, which included but were not limited to the City and Guilds of London Institute of

Science Technology and these courses jump-started my career as a laboratory technician. Over time, I was able to attain the position of laboratory technician, a position I held for almost seventeen years.

It was during those years that I met my husband, Emmanuel Taiwo, who was a dental student at the time. Our relationship blossomed and we eventually got married on October 3rd, 1981, after six years of courtship. Even though I knew my husband for six years before we got married, I did not introduce him to my parents until I was sure I was ready to spend the rest of my life with him, which is part of our culture. We have since been blessed with three wonderful children – Oluwatosin, meaning "God is worthy of praise"; Oluwakayode, meaning "God has brought us joy"; and Yewande, meaning "the return of my mother."

As time went on, Emmanuel became a dentist and he was practising at the medical college where I was also promoted to the position of laboratory technologist. Initially, I was satisfied with my job until one day the Dean of the School of Pharmacy where I worked made an insulting comment about technicians coming in to use the "Academic staff lounge." The University of Lagos College of Medicine had a strange policy at that time that only those with Bachelor's or Master's degrees or those who were lecturers were allowed into the lounge. Therefore, as an individual with only a college diploma, I was not entitled to be in there. The insulting statement from the dean reaffirmed this as he outrightly told those of us without a degree to vacate the lounge immediately. The statement hit me like a big knife in the chest. I was sad and upset as I ran out of the lounge and went home crying. Right on that day, I vowed to continue my education all the way to the Master's level and beyond.

As the next academic year came by, I applied to the part-time Bachelor's degree in biology at the University of Lagos. By the time I got in the following year, I had just given birth to my second child. My son was just a few months old when I started my courses towards this degree. At the same time, I continued my full-time job as a laboratory technician and despite this, I remained one of the top students in my class. I was more than determined to acquire the best grade possible so I could get into the Master's program. With determination, hard work and prayers, I completed my Bachelor's degree in five years and even had my third child around this same period. Despite the rigour, I still managed to finish with a cumulative GPA of 3.68, which put me in the second class upper division.

Not to be sidetracked by my accomplishment, I began my full-time Master's program in Medical Microbiology. With determination for success, I was still working full-time as a laboratory technologist and also juggling a home life with three young children. I was so determined that I would not allow anything to stand in the way of becoming a lecturer, I so much wanted to become a colleague of the same dean who had ridiculed me in the staff lounge years back. Fortunately for me, the department got a new dean, a God-fearing man who was very supportive and encouraging. I finished my Master's degree as the best student in the department, ending up with a cumulative GPA of 4.28 out of 5.

The Dean of the School of Pharmacy during this period was so impressed with my determination and performance that he encouraged me to publish a paper from my Master's thesis, so that I could use that as a springboard from my technical background into academics. As appealing as this sounded, it was not an easy endeavour since I was not trained as a pharmacist, and at that time, it would have been impossible for a non-pharmacy trained individual to become an instructor at the School of Pharmacy. However, the transition was a little easier because of my decade of technical instruction at the school. Consequently, I became a lecturer and taught Pharmaceutical Microbiology to the pharmacy students. My effort was crowned shortly before I made my transition into academics when I was awarded a Commonwealth Scholarship to Dalhousie University to study for another Master's degree.

I first came to Canada on September 1, 1995, to do a Master's degree in Microbiology and Immunology. Unfortunately, as excited as I was, due to various circumstances beyond my control I could not complete that degree, so I voluntarily withdrew and went back home to Nigeria. Before leaving for Nigeria, I had an ongoing patent research project with my supervisor. The project was on the "Antibacterial activities of the aqueous extract from Nigerian chewing sticks." Because of the patent, my supervisor continued to get in touch with me while I was back home in Nigeria and I continued to send him the materials needed for the research.

Let me briefly take you back to my short ten months' stay as a postgraduate student at Dalhousie. I withdrew from the program for so many personal reasons, but prominent among them was how unhappy I was as a student. I had no friends and for some reason, which I later perceived to be racially motivated, none of the white students wanted to have anything to do with me. I remember clearly in one of my undergraduate classes nobody would sit beside me or allow me to ask them questions when things were not clear to me. It was so bad that my supervisor advised me to always bring a tape recorder to lectures. The burden was so much on me – listening to tapes and writing out my notes before proceeding to studying. All of these, coupled with the alienation from my family back in Nigeria, stood in my way and became a deterrent to my success here in Canada. This resulted in my decision to withdraw and go back home to my family in Nigeria.

Back in Nigeria, I knew in my heart that I needed to do something for the future of my family and my children in particular. I wanted them to have it easier than I did; I wanted to open doors of opportunity for them to walk through. I remained committed to my project while back in Nigeria and continued to apply for various grants and sponsorships available there. Over time, I was fortunate to receive the United Nations Development Program Research Project Scholarship and I was able to return to Canada by the summer of 1998. On my return, I picked up my research project where I left off with my supervisor and was able to publish the project findings.

Sadly, my hope soon turned into a nightmare when the project suddenly came to a standstill due to lack of further funding. I sought various alternatives; I tried diverting from academics into other areas of microbiology but without any success (a result of being a foreign-trained professional). While contemplating what to do next, I decided to start a course in counselling skills through an International Correspondence School (Education Direct) in Quebec. I successfully completed all fourteen exams required within a period of one year and was awarded a diploma with distinction in counselling skills in May of 2000.

During this period, I applied for several jobs, but none was successful, not even with my Master's degree. I could not really understand if my failure was due to being a foreign student or because I was Black. Time went by and I was finally able to break the unemployment barrier when I secured a position as a personal care worker, a position from which I rose through the ranks to become a house manager within two months of employment. While at this job, I tried for four years to pursue various positions in the field of microbiology and medical sciences – a field in which I have been trained and acquired years of experience. Unfortunately, all attempts proved abortive.

As I continued to ponder my next move, I began to realize the unique role I have been playing in the social service industry. I began to see clearly the position of each client that I dealt with on a daily basis. I saw how empathy, love and understanding have been beneficial to many of my clients in being able to carry on with each day despite their condition. I saw myself as being a fundamental instrument in assisting them to cope with life's obstacles. I came to realize how unique each client was despite his or her disabilities. Having in-depth understanding of each diagnosis due to my background in the medical sciences, I was able to face the different challenges with ease. I was not only able to use the support perspective but also developed the skill of using strength and structural perspectives, therefore empowering my clients to be able to take up certain roles or skills in their daily living.

This is where I saw the ray of hope; this is where I reached a turning point in my life. In my quest for a career path I suddenly saw the light as I decided to focus on becoming other people's mentor, guide and confidant. Consequently, this resulted in my undaunted decision to become a social worker.

Choosing a new career was largely motivated by my current employment. Having to write this story gives me the opportunity to look back and acknowledge the fine gesture of my supervisor and director who saw my potential and gave me the opportunity to combine a full-time job with the social work studies.

I began to pursue the Bachelor of Social Work degree at Dalhousie University School of Social Work in September of 2003. I brought into this program various life skills that I have acquired both in my academic endeavours and in other areas of life.

My first year as a social work student was very challenging for various reasons. I have come from a completely different academic background. The terminology used in social work was different from that of microbiology. Also, things were more challenging working full-time and taking care of three children, but I was more determined to be successful in my quest.

Other challenges I faced in my first year at the School of Social Work were alienation from some of my colleagues, which caused me to feel excluded and not accepted. I withdrew to myself, and was unable to demonstrate my utmost potential. My feelings during those periods affected my participation, confidence and probably my attitude. I discovered that "whiteness" dominated the curriculum, the culture and the environment. To me, this was not a foreign concept. Since I came to Canada I realize that colour matters, which I never thought of while growing up in my country, but what I did not expect was the act of racism. I experienced racism on a daily basis both in school and in society at large. In spite of all these challenges, I was quite fortunate to have some wonderful and helpful professors, and some caring and understanding classmates. I am very grateful for their encouragement and assistance, which has enabled me to continue on this great journey. With the assistance of a NSASW bursary, my family and friends and with lots of determination and hard work I successfully completed my first year and continued the journey into the second year of the program.

At the beginning of second year, the feeling of exclusion still persisted even though I was doing very well in my courses. I continued to feel this alienation until the occurrence of circumstances at the School of Social Work which caused me to challenge the system of white privilege and racism. The whole situation brought back the memory of my experience when I first came to Dalhousie in 1995.

Fortunately, when the issue of racism and white privilege became an open topic of discussion, the barrier was broken. It was then that I had the opportunity to let out my feelings and thoughts. According to the theory of cognitive behaviour, the ability to express inner feelings and thoughts can result in positive behaviour, and this was what happened to me: letting out my positive behaviour. I had the opportunity to share my past knowledge or struggles without the fear of being judged.

The opening of this crucial topic led to the creation of the caucus groups. There is no doubt in my mind that these groups have brought about a positive action which might bring total change in the colonization of Dalhousie's School of Social Work and subsequently the institution in general in the near future. The most exciting part of this journey is how so many of my white colleagues became conscious of the fact that they might have been an oppressor in the past and were willing to change, to try to be an ally or advocate in bridging the gap between whites and people of colour.

My program continues for the next year and, God willing, I intend to pursue my Master's degree as soon as I am able to get into the social work field, a journey that looks far away and full of fear.

The fact remains that I am still a Black woman, a visible yet invisible minority and an immigrant. What the future holds for me, I do not know, but one thing is clear: I will never give up until the battle is won, until I am able to prove that everybody has the right in this world to become what they want as long as they do not give up or give in to defeat.

In conclusion, I will acknowledge that even though racial differences may pose formidable challenges to social work practice, and the racially dissimilar social worker and client might approach each other with little understanding of each other's social realities, it is still the duty of social workers to work out the process of decolonization. Each social worker or colleague should critically examine the breadth of his or her own exposure to minority communities and culture. As McDonald states, "If this exposure is limited they should seek and obtain inter-ethnic experience. It is unprofessional if clients are to take the burden of educating their social workers about the realities of racial injustice" (McDonald, 2005, as cited in Taiwo, 2005, p. 9).

Finally, the journey so far has helped me to realize how important it is to be an ally in bridging the gap and resisting racism. If everyone who has experienced racism, loneliness and struggles for being a minority takes this positive step, this will surely be helpful in the future of our social work practice. Therefore, according to Janet Pothier (2005, p. 1):

> It is important for each one of us to remember as we embark on this journey in social work, the discomfort we often experience is not a bad thing, it is not something to hide from, but it is something to be embraced, loved and nurtured and to explore because from this discomfort comes new found understanding of self and awareness of how white privilege has served to oppress others. Some of us will experience more pain than others; some of us may never complete the journey (as cited in Taiwo, 2005, p. 10).

I will therefore say to those of you who are white that you may escape the effect and the pain of racial discrimination, but to those of us who are "racially visible" we might never escape; we might have to live under the cloak of whiteness our entire lives. But one thing is sure by the power of the Almighty God, I will surely sail through. One day I will see the light at the end of the tunnel, and this light would continue to reflect my ray of hope.

References

Fadipe, N.A. (1970). *The sociology of the Yoruba*. Ibadan. Nigeria: University Press.

Oduma Magazine 3(2) December 1977, p. 13.

Gordon, R. G., Jr. (Ed) (2005). *Ethnologue: Languages of the world*, Fifteenth edition. Dallas, Texas. SIL International. Online Version: http://www.ethnologue.com/. Retrieved February 21, 2006.

Pothier, J. (2004). *As long as he's not Black, Catholic or French: Examining whiteness*. Dalhousie University School of Social Work. Unpublished paper.

Taiwo, O.A. (2005). Critical reflection and synthesis paper: "White privilege and racism." Dalhousie School of Social Work, Halifax. Unpublished paper.

Chapter 13

Learning to See the Best of Both Worlds

Erin Desmond

I was born March 21, 1976, to two African Nova Scotian parents. I was a beautiful Black baby girl lying in the old Grace Maternity Hospital in Halifax, Nova Scotia. My mum, a young teen with no means to raise or support me, had made a hard decision. Without consulting my birth father, she chose to place me for adoption. At that time the laws usually favoured the mother when making adoption decisions, especially when the parents were not married. And so I began my journey in my permanent home.

After my mother made the decision to give me up, I was moved from the hospital to the first of two foster homes. This was too far away for her to visit and so I was moved to one closer. She visited me until my adoptive parents legally adopted me. My file number was 7602003551. My new parents applied to the government of Canada to adopt me on May 27, 1976. I was legally adopted on June 11, 1976, and was brought home with my adoptive parents.

I was told that I was special because I was an African Nova Scotian baby who was adopted by white parents. This was virtually unheard of in 1976 because most people looked to adopt same race babies, and the adoption agencies liked to sustain same race adoptions. Although placing children in good homes was a priority for the Department of Community Services (DCS) and other adoption agencies, race played a central role at that time. One example is the following statement found in my adoption report, recorded by a social worker working with DCS at the time: "Erin does not show her Black heritage, she looks more South American or Hawaiian rather than Black, although she is supposedly full Black."

After I read that statement, I was extremely upset. I felt the comments were condescending, rude, and racist. The evidence was recorded and they had had visual confirmation, yet they still noted that I did not show my heritage. I feel that there was a general perception that Blacks are supposed to be extremely dark, not taking into consideration that Black people come in many different shades and colours of brown and black. What is my heritage supposed to look like? Black as tar? Black as night? Black as the ace of spades? How should I look? Maxine Tynes says it best in her book *Save the World for Me*. Her poem "The Profile of Africa" states, "we people of colour, brown, black, tan, coffee, coffee cream, ebony . . . beautiful, strong, exotic in profile" (p. 63). The comment, to me, reflected the underlying racist opinions, attitudes and misconceptions about Black people. The thought also passed through my mind that they did not want to present me as being Black and this would improve my chances for adoption if I were not Black but of another ancestry.

My mother has told me many stories over the years about how she has been questioned, looked at by people who seemed to be surprised and rather curious when they saw her toting around a Black baby. Even now, when I call for her when we are out together or I introduce her as my mum, people look in amazement and utter confusion. It has never dawned on people, even to this day, that a Black child can have white parents or that white parents can have a Black child. And people say that race does not matter. Obviously race does matter.

I began to ask questions about skin colour and my adoption when I began day care at around three or four years old. This was when people would make comments and I was old enough to ask questions and have my feelings hurt by the insensitivity and subtle acts of racism of others. It hurt but I was always strong and had a lot of emotional supports to help me deal with the racially motivated incidents that have occurred in my lifetime. My supports included my primary family group. My mum was there to help calm me down after any racist incident and to help me deal with my anger. My dad was there too. He would remind me that not everyone acts or thinks as a racist person. He reminds me that he works to help make people change their ideas, words and actions concerning people of other cultures. I had support from my friends, many of whom were not white and many who were not racist people. We would talk about the situations, my feelings, and reactions and they gave their insight as well.

I always had everything I needed. I always had love, education, discipline, food and opportunity. I have been privileged enough to be enrolled in swimming, skating, gymnastics, piano, organ, dance, ballet, and jazz classes. I have had the comforts and luxuries afforded by the upper-middle-class lifestyle in travel, good food and opportunity. I have travelled extensively throughout Canada, the United States, Australia, New Zealand, Cuba, Bermuda, and Hawaii. I had always loved to learn about different cultures as well as my own. I have always been made to feel I was just one of the kids in the family growing up. I am the eldest of four. I have two younger sisters (one of whom is also Black and adopted from another family) and a brother. I have always been surrounded by people, not Black or white people, just people who cared for us and us for them.

As I grew up and became increasingly aware of racism and race consciousness, things became very polarized around issues of Black and white. For example, people at school made it clear: you date people in your own race. They are my friends but I am still a little different because my skin is brown and theirs is white. Your family is white, but why are you Black? Nigger, Negro, coloured, Black, African Canadian – I've heard it all before. There's always someone around to remind me of who I am on the outside.

I've had a lot of racist experiences in my life. Being followed around stores was a regular occurrence. I've been followed by police and pulled over once for suspicion of bank machine robbery and I was stopped by police on another occasion because I left my cousin's house late at night (she lives near Gottingen Street) and as I passed four drug dealers on the corner, the police assumed that I was engaging in illegal activity, with no proof of this. When I was in Australia in 1989, people stared, followed me around stores, didn't want to serve me and generally had a cold attitude towards my sister and me. I initially wondered why that happened, then realized that Australians are familiar with Aboriginals, their native people who are Black, and my sister and I did not fit into this category. It has been said that what people don't understand, they fear and this fear can cause irrational behaviour. When I was in grade six, I dated a white boy at my elementary school and both the Black and white students were very intolerant of our mixed race relationship. In that same year, a fellow classmate got mad at me and called me a nigger. Unfortunately, people still hold negative assumptions of Black people and this translates into inequality for me and other Black people.

I did have the best of both worlds. My parents took the time to have books, movies, talks with me, friends and educational materials that highlighted mixed-race families, acceptance and respect. Most of the material came from England and the United States, not from Canada. So I was armed, and it did help me to deal with racist people and situations across my life span.

In addition to the ways in which my parents taught me to feel pride about my race, my mum always told me I had a fascination with my own adoption story and had her tell it to me over and over again. I had the fascination with my own roots and the roots of Black people and I wanted to learn as much as possible about it. I also discovered the book and film *Roots* by Alex Haley, and watched it over and over. My mum eventually bought me the series.

I have lived in Halifax most of my life, except for two years in Ottawa when I was a toddler. My mum is from the United States and my dad from Mount Thom, Nova Scotia. The melding of two very different worlds made for a flamboyant upbringing, especially as I entered my teen years.

In addition to the challenges of being raised in a racially mixed family, by white parents, I have also experienced a lot of other challenges in my short lifetime – my youngest sister being ill, my parents separating and then divorcing, changing the make up of our family. My mum becoming ill, being hospitalized and having surgery was stressful. That was the scariest time in my life. I coped with my mother's illness with tears. I cried so much. I talked to friends and family but it was so upsetting. It did help, however, that I was the oldest and took care of my younger siblings, so I pulled it together for them and that helped to deal better with my emotions and fears.

When my parents divorced I was actually joyful. It's not always good to stay together for the kids because it causes turmoil, stress, sadness, anger and fear. So when it ended I was happy. My dad moved out and the four of us stayed at our childhood home with our mother. Almost immediately, the house was happier, more relaxed and we were definitely relieved that the fighting, tension and negative atmosphere was no longer in the home. We all chipped in to help our mum and it worked out very well. We still saw our dad but we did not all have to live together and this was a good thing. Space is necessary sometimes to improve relationships and we all got along much better after my parents separated.

As I grew older and matured a little bit, I began to see where my parents were coming from. A new perspective is interesting and I definitely had lots to think about concerning my personal choices, how I wanted to live my life and how I was going to change. Luckily, I had a mother who gave me room to explore but always had a loving heart and sobering words to get me back on track.

I successfully made it through the public school system, graduating with good marks, as a bilingual person and with high hopes of going to Dalhousie to begin my university career. I graduated from Dalhousie with my first degree in 1997 – a Bachelor of Arts in Sociology and Social Anthropology. I went on to complete a second degree at Mount Saint Vincent University in 2003 – a Bachelor of Applied Arts in Family Studies and Gerontology. I loved what I learned and felt I had found what I wanted to pursue as a career, to work with seniors in the areas of advocacy and/or policy-making within the government or private practice.

Unfortunately, neither gave me any opportunities to enter into a career. I've since learned that completing a degree will not always yield good work opportunities in the field of your choice. Fortunately, again I had my mum there and we talked about different options I had to explore and different roads I could take to figure out what I wanted and needed to do to be able to have a happy and fulfilling career that I would love. I am currently pursuing a Bachelor of Social Work degree at the School of Social Work at Dalhousie University.

Becoming a single parent was another challenge I had to overcome. On June 23, 2003, I delivered a healthy baby girl, with very little time to prepare because I had severe medical issues, was on heavy doses of medications and discovered I was pregnant about three weeks before I delivered. And, yes, this does happen – it happened to me. It was extremely hard because I was not emotionally, psychologically, mentally, physically, spiritually, or financially prepared for a baby. If it were not for my mum, and all of my family and friends, I would not have been successful as a single parent.

As an adoptee, I always wondered about my birth families. Did I look like them? Did I act like them? Would we get along after we met? Why was I adopted? Why didn't they want me? These were all questions I needed answered, and they were when I met my birth father. My mum supported me one hundred percent in my search and subsequent reunion. She wanted to help me and was aware that I always wanted to meet my birth families. She was there to listen to the stories of all my reunions with my many family members. She looked at pictures, asked questions and matched similar details of my adoption story. She was truly happy for me. My dad was happy for me too. He knew I always wanted to meet my birth families. It was so funny, the things in common both my fathers had. They were both named Wayne. They had actually met years previously in meetings.

I met my birth father in January 1996. It was one of the happiest days of my life. In order to get to that day, it took many, many months of communication and work with a social worker.

When I was nineteen, I re-entered the adoption process through the Department of Community Services (DCS). First you are assigned your adoption reunion register number. You then get a letter from your social worker telling you that your parent or parents are looking for you. You contact your social worker to tell them whether or not you want to meet your parent(s). If your answer is no, a letter stating you do not want to meet them is sent to the birth parent(s) and the file is closed until you change your mind. If you respond yes, you proceed through the process of meeting your birth parent(s). You are then asked to write a non-identifying letter, as are your birth parent(s). This letter tells them about your interests, likes, dislikes, experiences, feelings, your life. You are not allowed to give any identifying information like your name, address, phone numbers or e-mail address. Your social worker ensures this by reading the letters you have sent to each other. The letters are then delivered.

Then you are each asked if you want to continue the process and if the answer is no, then again it is finished. If you answer yes, the process continues and you're asked to write a letter with identifying information. This letter can include names, addresses, phone numbers and e-mail addresses. Once those are exchanged all parties involved usually call each other to arrange for an in-person meeting. At this point your social worker's services are no longer needed; the meeting is the final step in the adoption reunification process and your file is closed. The relationship is now under your control and you are in charge of how the relationship will proceed.

In the cases that only one parent is searching and the birth child wants to meet the other birth parent, the parent you have met must sign a letter stating that they give permission for the file to be opened to obtain information concerning the other parent. You must pay a $50 fee to DCS for them to complete the search.

The results are then sent to your social worker and the information about the second parent is then released.

On July 24, 1995, I received a letter from my social worker telling me that my father had been looking for me since I was ten years old and that he wanted to meet me. This was memorable for my social worker for two reasons: one, because very few birth fathers look for their children and two, because they rarely begin to look for them at such a young age. Unfortunately, because my adoption was closed, there was no way for him to access any identifying information that would have helped him to find me. And so the process began.

The most notable change in adoption is that now they can be open and this allows for varying degrees of involvement of the birth parents in the lives of the child they have given up and of the adoptive parents. Involvement can be anything from receiving letters and pictures to being physically present and attending special events like birthdays or holidays.

My personal process to meet my birth parents was extensive. After we exchanged the identifying letters, read them, and talked with the social worker we were finally allowed to talk on the phone. The anticipation of the phone call was almost too much for me to bear. I was so nervous and excited I thought I would be sick. The phone rang and it was my birth father on the other end of the line.

He was so kind and happy to finally talk to me after all these years. He wasted no time telling me he loved me and that he had wanted to keep and raise me but my birth mother hadn't wanted that. He related how he had come to the hospital one day to visit me and I was gone; how that made him so angry and sad. He exclaimed many times during our talk, "My baby, my baby girl." It was so good to hear. I had so many questions, twenty years of questions. My birth father, luckily, was ready for me and we talked and talked and talked. I internalized his voice; I never want to forget his voice. He had the key to my biological being. He had the other side of the adoption story that I never knew. He was my dad. We planned to meet before the end of our conversation, and we did so on January 31, 1996.

January 31st came so fast. I was so excited to meet my birth father. He came to my house to pick me up. He met my adoptive mum and my two sisters and brother. They talked for a few minutes and then we got into his car. We just stared at each other, examining each other's faces, trying to find a family resemblance. "Does she have any of my features?" "Do I have any of his?"

"I've always wondered what you'd look like. I always looked for you on the streets when I went out, trying to spot you in the crowd," my dad told me almost immediately. He also told me that he didn't want me placed for adoption, that he alone would not have been able to raise me but with help he would have tried. He had a plan for me to be raised jointly with him, his mom, and his many older sisters who were ready, willing and able to help him out. Not to mention, he would have had the benefit of living in North Preston and having family there who could play a larger role of raising me under their belief that it takes a village to raise a child. My birth mother, however, didn't like that idea.

I cried. I felt so happy and relieved that we had finally met; I was learning my birth story. It felt so good to be wanted and to learn his truth that he had never wanted me to be placed for adoption. To finally feel, know and hear that my dad loved me and called me his baby because I was and am his baby girl. He remembered me as a baby, and even as an adult I was still his baby. I had waited for twenty years to hear those words.

After this initial contact, I went to meet the rest of his family. I was nervous but so excited to finally meet everyone. We arrived at his house and I met his wife, two daughters, and his oldest sister, who was like his mum. They were so kind and welcoming and I was so warmly received, I felt like I belonged. I'd finally met the family I'd been wondering about for twenty years. From that day on, I continued to meet people from my family, talk with my dad, share with my dad and just soak him in. He is part of me and I am part of him.

My dad gave me something very special soon after we met – a gold ring. He wore this ring on his finger daily since the day he discovered I was placed for adoption without his consent, the day he had his heart broken, when his baby girl was gone with no chance of finding me. This ring represented all his anger, turmoil, sadness, grief, despair, loss, hope and faith of someday reuniting with me. He gave me this ring and I've worn it everyday since. I wear it to honour him, me, and our new relationship together as father and daughter.

I met my birth mother in August 1996. The Black communities in Nova Scotia are small enough that someone always knows someone else and I heard she wanted to meet me. I was able to get her number through my birth father and I called her. We talked for a little while and arranged to meet. I was given the phone number of my aunt, my birth mother's only sister, and I phoned her too. I was scared to phone them both, but my birth father supported me and knew I wanted to meet her. I talked to my aunt, and she made a good impression on me by actually spelling my name correctly, by being so interested in me and offering her house as the meeting place.

My adoptive mum drove me there and I remember my birth family looking out the window watching me pull up in the driveway. I got inside and we all just looked at each other. My birth mother took me into her arms and hugged me so tight. I moved into the living room where I met two of my aunts, one of my uncles, three of my birth sisters and four of my cousins. We all cried, laughed, watched each other, and talked. We all sounded like chickens in a henhouse, everyone talking and screaming at the same time. We all had so much to say and so many questions to ask each other. Our first meeting had gone so well and I was happy and relieved that we all got along. I felt that I was loved and cared for and that this was the beginning of a beautiful lifelong relationship between my maternal birth family and me. All was well, or so I thought.

Unfortunately, the lustre didn't last. As time passed and I learned more about my birth mother and sisters, the more complex our relationship became. True personality traits began to emerge. I did not know people like this – people whose lives are always in turmoil, always in crises. Needless to say, the stress levels began to rise. My maternal birth family is laden with problems. I was not used to this. I was beginning to see why the Good Lord ensured my adoption, to relieve me from an upbringing that would have been steeped in chaos and confusion.

I discovered that my birth mother really could not have cared less if she met me or not. I was told she wanted to meet me because she had heard rumours of someone who looked like her, to the point where people were confusing us, and out of curiosity she wanted to meet me. Shock, sadness, disappointment, hurt, rage – all these feelings rolled through my body. The fantasy reunions so often portrayed on television, which I had internalized, were shattered by the harsh reality that my own mum, the woman who gave birth to me, really did not want me. I definitely was not prepared for that.

So with my feelings and negative experiences I was having with my birth mother and sisters, I had to seek counselling to deal with my feelings and emotional distress. Finally, I decided to cut communication completely with my birth mother, and partially with my birth sisters. I would have never predicted this would happen, but it was something I had to do to protect myself and maintain my sanity.

I did not talk to my birth mother at all for a few years. However, when I moved to New York in 2000, a turning point in our relationship occurred because we began to communicate again via letters. My birth mother wrote to me a heartfelt apology and asked if we could start over again. From 2000 onward, we have slowly been rebuilding our relationship.

One good lesson I have learned in the whole process of meeting, getting to know and maintaining a relationship with both birth parents and the multitudes of family that come with them, is that you cannot expect to have happen to you what you see on television. That magical wonderland, which is perfect when portrayed in fiction, just does not happen that way all the time in reality. Reunification can be difficult and challenging for adopted children and their birth families, and relationships need to be nurtured and developed; they do not happen in a vacuum.

As noted previously, I hold two degrees: a BA in sociology from Dalhousie and a Bachelor's of Applied Arts in family studies and gerontology from the Mount. Unfortunately, family studies and gerontology is a newly emerging field of study; therefore, employment opportunities are limited because the gerontology degree is extremely broad and not focused on specific skills. To my disappointment, I was not able to secure solid employment with these degrees, so I decided to redirect my focus to social work.

This social work degree allows me to build on what I have learned in my two previous degrees. I can combine and use my knowledge and education that will enable me to work in private practice, not-for-profit or government agencies to help seniors, women, people of colour or in adoption services. I am extremely happy that I decided to pursue this degree and in doing so, I am preparing myself to help others.

My interest in social work is also rooted in my own personal life experiences. The first experience is my own adoption. Why are particular policies in place? Can they change? Are they for the best interest of all parties involved? Is race consciousness still at the forefront of adoptions in contemporary society? If yes, why? If not, why not? Is racism and race consciousness stopping potential adoptive parents from finding children they want to love and raise? These have been questions and issues that I have thought of for many years.

The second experience that led me to a career in social work was the removal of two of my nephews and one of my nieces from one of my maternal birth sisters. This was so hard on everyone, and it really exposed me to the current system of child protection. Things happened quickly, as they should, but the process did not adequately address some issues that arose such as appropriate foster care, looking for family to help in providing shelter in the short term, visitation, adoption, and medical care for the children. I felt the system lacked the appropriate checks for foster parents, and sufficient culturally sensitive training of the social workers involved in this case. I felt they really needed to pay more attention to the needs of the children in terms of family stability and their receiving of appropriate physical, mental, emotional and psychological counselling. This experience motivated me to pursue a social work career and to work hard to effect change in policy, education and practice. I am also interested in international adoption. I think there is a need to simply match children who need loving parents with parents who can provide a stable, supportive and caring environment for these children. Adoption within Canada is complicated and many are looking to adopt children from other countries.

I want to be an example to others that racially blended families that offer love, support, caring, understanding, and an open mind can produce a well-rounded, capable, intelligent person. My parents taught me to be happy with who I am, that I am the only one who defines who I am and to not be defined by other people. They also taught me that I am capable and worthy of all that life has to offer as long as I'm willing to work for it, and that the world is a big place and that there is a lot of opportunity in the world and to not limit myself. Only I can limit myself.

In addition, my parents taught me to have a positive self and racial identity. Black is beautiful. From them, I learned that I should be proud to be Black and that I come from a long line of strong, Black people. They told me that I have the same inner strength that my ancestors carried with them. They nurtured my passion for genealogy, Black history, and history in general and how this speaks directly to people living in the world today. They raised me to realize that there are racist people everywhere in the world, but that I have as much right as anyone else on this earth to be anywhere I want to be and to not cower under the racist impositions of others. They always reminded me that I have to learn to ignore these people and realize and understand that people are raised in many different ways. If something happened that causes your civil or human rights to be violated, fight for your rights as a human being and Canadian citizen. Education is extremely important and is useful in helping me to learn new things, helping others learn by sharing what I've learned with them. Education can make a difference for me in this world.

I am still interested in working with seniors. To advocate for their rights as human beings and to help seniors not be marginalized in a society where youth is epitomized as ideal are goals I would like to pursue. There is a lot of work that needs to be done to help seniors enjoy their lives with full participation in society without being seen as a burden.

As I begin my career in social work, I hope to effect and affect positive change for the people that I will be working with, whether it is with children or seniors. I want to help people empower themselves to live a better life. I know upon my graduation I will be able to find a job helping people. I feel that I am capable of this and will work hard to fulfill my dream.

My journey has been full and interesting. I have experienced many emotional, social, psychological, spiritual changes and I don't think I'd change a thing. Out of every experience, you grow, learn and it effects who you are. I've learned a lot in the classroom of life, the classrooms of universities and the classrooms of my Lord, and I know good and bad. I think that I have experienced so much it will help me to relate to people better in my social work career. I will be able to relate to the single parent, to women, to Black people, to adoptees who balance both birth and adoptive families and their dynamics, to people who are living in the low-income bracket and to people who have had spiritual and religious roller coaster rides. I will be able to relate to people who have lived with overt and covert racism all their lives as I have.

All of these experiences will help me to be real with my clients, to be a better survivor. My aspiration is to be able to help increasingly diverse groups of people as their social worker, and to help other social workers – current and yet to come – be accepting of all people.

References

Tynes, Maxine. (1991). *Save the world for me*. Lawrencetown Beach, Nova Scotia, Canada: Pottersfield Press.

Province of Nova Scotia Department of Community Services Nov. 5, 1976 – Adoption study final report.

Chapter 14

My Journey to Health and Becoming Visible

Phyllis Marsh-Jarvis

Invisible
I walked in silence and in fear
Shuddering at her mad looking stare
There was no one around me to care!
The pain and hurt that she caused me
No one around me chose to see
Purple and black bruises
Hid from the eye
The thick black strap that made me cry
Cruel words that lingered in my heart
Creating my desire from this world to depart
The system failed me, leaving me on my own
A child, motherless and alone
The only place that I felt safe
Was in my make belief hiding space
This question I am left to face
Will I ever fit the human race
The system left me a lonely place
Invisible

"I was invisible; no one came to rescue me!"

My apartment echoes dead silence. Breaking that silence are the muffled voices of my ghosts from the past. Hauntingly, they whisper over and over again, "invisible child, invisible child." I fight back, heartening myself to an affirmative space. I am healed, I have moved on. I am the epitome of an abuse survivor. I will not wallow in the past.

But, alas, today I am not afforded the luxury of reassurance, self-confidence or self-cleansing. No, today is that heartwrenching time of memories, painful memories. Today is Mother's Day. As with every Mother's Day for me, it comes with a price. It manifests deep feelings of hurt, fear, loathing, anger, loss, regret, feelings of being invisible, and unanswered questions.

Those questions simply stated: Why? Why was I placed in such a lonely space? Why was I left invisible? Why did no one come to rescue me? Why could they not see my pain? Why should I forgive them?

The feel of steam from my cup of herbal tea, which is ironically called "spiced taste of sweet memories," dances on my forehead as hot tears stream down my face and form around my lips. At this point I have no fight, no recourse. I begrudgingly surrender to the moment.

The memories . . .

Eighty-six Tupper St.

Phone number 564-5255

The big concrete step that framed the front of the store

The wooden bench that was both prison and fun

The milk crate on the step (her daily throne)

The smell of salt ribs and pig tails from their resting place, the pickle barrel in the store

The smell of dustbane-swept floors

The tedious task of stocking store shelves while my friends were outside playing

The succulent smell of her fried fish on Wednesday

The crisp sharp suffocating fangs of tension always in the air

The aroma of her black-eyed peas and roast chicken in spicy tomato gravy on Sunday

The voice of Anne Terry's commentary on CJCB, I wanted to grow up and be like her someday

The smell of my own fear: stomach-curdling, leg-trembling, fist-clenching fear

"I was invisible; no one came to rescue me!"

Beginnings

I was adopted at the age of three and a half years old. I can still remember vividly my first encounter with "motherhood." My adoptive mother was standing in front of the bureau dresser mirror. I watched this strange but beautiful woman priming herself. She was in a white slip with lots of pretty lace. Around her neck was a beautiful strand of pearls (which I still have). She paid no mind to me for a long time. It was as though I was invisible. I was frightened and nervous, but I wanted her to say something nice to me.

Without warning she turned around and made an ugly face. My little heart raced in fear. Her lips began to move. The words have stayed with me clearly and deeply all of these years: "I hate you, I don't want you." I sat stuck to the chair. My belly button felt funny. It felt like it was telling me something but I didn't know what it was saying and I wanted that feeling to go away.

That belly button feeling is a seventh sense to me now in my daily life.

I sat still. She turned back to the mirror, powdered her face and put on a beautiful black dress and black high heel shoes. She left the room. I timidly followed her. She said nothing to me. I was invisible to her.

These spoken words seem to set the tone for the relationship between my adoptive mother and me for the next fifteen years.

The abuse was progressive, and the older I got the more intense the degradation. I was always terrified. As a little girl when she would call my name I would run to see what she wanted, all the while hoping I had done nothing wrong to warrant a beating. Three main incidents come to my mind that demonstrate my daily torment, and they remain strong images in my mind.

We had a store and our living quarters were in the back of this establishment. When Violet (Vi) would beat me, people in the store could hear me screaming, but no one ever came to my assistance. I do remember my last beating with that horrible strap. My god-mother Mae, who was doing her weekly grocery shopping, came upstairs where Vi was savagely beating me. She stopped her and told her if she ever beat me again she would have to deal with her. This was a little too late; unfortunately, the years of beatings had taken their toll, and the emotional and psychological damage had already been done.

By the way, the beatings from that point escalated from the strap to the fists. I would be thrown down on the floor and pummeled fiercely with her fists. With every blow a piece of me died, until there was no Phyllis and I became an empty shell. I think I remember that moment – she was beating me and I did not feel the blows anymore. I would just stare at her. I don't know what she saw, but she would yell at me to stop looking at her, but I wouldn't. I had become numb, hateful and defiant. I remember I would not cry. I refused to let her know she was hurting me. I think I was at the point where I couldn't hurt anymore. There was no more hurt left inside me. Hatred and defiance replaced my hurt. It is at this point that my emotions became entangled; love and hate became my struggle and hate won. This was around the age of nine or ten.

Despite her cruelty I always wanted her approval. One of my duties at a very early age (from about seven) was to help out in our grocery store. My adoptive parents' expectations of me were high and left little room for error.

This day the store was quite crowded and I thought I would show Vi my best. A good friend of mine came in for some cooked ham. I had seen my adoptive father use the new slicer he bought, but I was never taught how to use it. I sliced the ham and was so proud of myself. Surely today I will win her favour, I thought. After all, I am helping her. I anxiously and proudly showed her the ham, knowing she was going to be pleased. Immediately I saw that look. I became panic-stricken. What did I do wrong? I just sliced the ham. Why was she upset?

In my eagerness to please her, I did not adjust the slicer. I did not know I had to adjust the slicer. I cut the ham too thick. She was relentless in her attack. She grabbed the stick that we used to take things off the high shelf, turned it to the sharp steel point and drove it in my leg. The crowded store went silent. No one came to my assistance.

I bent to the floor writhing in pain. I slowly looked at my leg and was shocked to see white things were hanging out from a deep imbedded hole. There was blood flowing. I began to shake and felt sick to my stomach.

A woman named Blanche finally said, " Eleazer is coming and I am going to tell him." She turned to my mother and said, "I don't care if you beat me, but I am telling Elly." With that Blanche disappeared. My mother hollered at me and said, "Straighten up, and stand on your feet." My dad, returning from town, came rushing in to see what happened. I showed him my leg. He didn't speak. He picked me up, put me in the car and took me to our doctor.

The hole was so deep it could not be stitched. Dr. Calder packed it with dressing. The one thing I remember the doctor saying, which I did not understand at the time, was "How long are you going to let this go on, Eleazer?" They turned from me, walked to another part of his office and spoke softly so I could not hear.

The worst experience of these atrocities was the day she tried to drown me in the toilet bowl. I have tried for years to remember the offence I committed that would warrant such a barbarous punishment. I remember her dragging me to the bathroom, forcing me to the floor and pushing my head in the toilet bowl several times.

Each time my face went in the water, I choked and I truly thought I was going to die. When she was finished she just left me there, gasping what I felt was for my life. She did not come back to see if I was okay; I think that day I wished I had died. I stayed upstairs for a long time. I think she finally ordered me down for supper. I remember feeling worthless, hopeless and empty. The memory of this incident still makes me sad. It hurts to know that someone could hold me in such contempt, and I always ponder what would have happened if I had died. I wonder if she would have felt anything at that time. All I ever wanted from her was her love and approval, but "I was invisible; no one came to rescue me!"

Pivotal Life Moments

A climactic pivotal moment in my life was discovering I was an adopted child. This information came from blameless malicious child play of which I was the originator. I was playing outside with my friend Carol. We got into an argument and I made an insulting comment about her father. She of course responded with the "big secret" – "At least my mother and father are my real parents." Stunned by her comment I immediately retorted, "And so are mine." Carol was like the cat that swallowed the canary. She smugly repeated the secret again. That was it. I was going to get her in trouble for telling terrible lies. I ran in the house to tell Vi what she said.

The next few moments changed my life forever. She told me to go into the store and bring the newspaper. I did. I was about ten years old, I believe. She told me to open to a certain page. On that page there were babies, Black babies, and it talked about adoption. She blankly stated, "That's where you come from." She gave no other explanation. There was no hug. There was no warmth. I was in shock. I was mortified. I ran out of the house. I cried and cried and cried. My heart was racing, my throat was dry and the tears seemed to burn into my face. It could not be true, though. People said I looked like her, but she is nothing to me? She beat me, but she is nothing to me? Why? Why? I wanted to run away from there immediately. I had nowhere to go, nowhere to hide, no one to take me!

"I was invisible; no one came to rescue me!"

I think about the social worker who placed me in this home. I visualize her going home after my placement and telling her husband she had the best day ever. I picture them sharing a glass of wine together to celebrate what she believed was the best placement of her career. After all, she found a family who could meet my needs. I would be fed properly, definitely clothed in the best and I had a clean home. She was able to swell with pride because she had taken care of my needs.

She missed it! Her placement made me invisible; her joy was my fall into the depths of toxic dysfunction. What's sad is she moved on without knowing the damage she perpetuated in my life. I have longed to confront her and tell her my pain over the years. I want the opportunity to ask her what she would have done differently if she had seen me. More than that, I want to know what she saw when she came to visit at the home of my adoptive parents. What was her perception of that little girl sitting and trembling on that wooden chair? Did she see me?

For the longest while when I did presentations to women regarding abuse and survival I would tell them my story and claim there was no social worker involved. It took a while for me to realize I had blocked her completely out of my memory. There was a woman; she was tall and carried a briefcase. I think I remember a black coat. I don't remember her name nor do I remember her face. I know she did come.

When she came to the house I was always made to sit in the wooden chair next to the banister. I was schooled by Vi not to open my mouth. The lady would speak to Vi and never directed any questions to me. To my memory the social worker hardly looked at me. If she did look at me, what did she see? I was a sitting vision of fear, hurt and pain. My body language illuminated my story without me speaking, but I was invisible to her. This social worker was instrumental in approving this adoption without seeing the texture of me, which she ignored. She did not serve the best interest of this child. I long to confront her negligence.

"I was invisible; she did not come back to rescue me!"

The last straw came for me with Vi when she told me she was not going to beat me with her fists anymore.

She told me she was going to use the knife that we kept at the side of the kitchen sink. (This was a black-handled knife with a long blade that she used for cutting meat and cleaning fish.) Those words ripped at my belly button. Instinctively, I knew I was fighting for my life.

It was at that moment, despite the hardships I had faced, that I wanted to live. I needed to take my life back. It was my first step to freedom. Calmly, I told her that if she attacked me with the knife I would fight back and I would be the winner. I also told her when I finished school that year I was going to Toronto and I wasn't coming back. I was so afraid when these words had come out of my mouth that I couldn't feel my body. I expected her to rush at me, but instead she shocked me with her response.

In a quiet voice she simply stated that in all the years I was with her that was the first time I had talked back to her. I immediately felt a surge of power. I told her I was not going to let her hurt me anymore. With that I turned on my heels and walked into the store to relate to my dad what happened and tell him my decision to leave and not return. He immediately began to cry. I loved him passionately, but through my years of pain he did nothing to help me. He loved me but sacrificed me to her cruelty, I believe to protect her. He had a boundless devotion to Vi that took precedence at any cost.

"I was invisible; no one came to rescue me!"

Entering A Mud Puddle . . . Mother's Day

Today is a day when mothers are honoured. They will be taken out to dinner, relieved from their regular motherly household duties, have breakfast in bed and be lavished with all the love and attention a mother deserves. Why? Because mothers are naturally nurturing and loving. They honourably and humbly fulfill the role of protector. I ask myself, why am I sitting here this Mother's Day, like other Mother's Days in the past, empty? I sit here wrestling and aimlessly grasping to feel something. Nothing happens.

My spiritual heart is void. My inner cup is empty. I don't understand my lack of consciousness that comes with this personal crisis. After all, I won my freedom years ago. I found my power and I have moved on.

The truth be told, when I thought I had gained my freedom I had actually arrived at my road to bondage. This bondage was the fallout from my childhood abuse; I would travel this road for about twenty-three years. This journey was a "stuck in the mud" notion. On Mother's Day I feel that I wander back to the beginning of that mud puddle. The mud is my guilt and my feelings of void. The void is the longing for my mother's love; the guilt is my personal failure as a mother. You see, I became Vi's specimen. I hadn't even noticed.

My desire is to pull myself out of the mud permanently. If I could only face that social worker! I pause from my thoughts. I close my eyes. Silently I pray, "Lord, you need to lift this burden from me. I need you to set my ragged soul free. Help me, Lord." The words of a hymn come to mind:

Take me back, take me back, dear Lord
To the place where I first received you.
Take me back, take me back, dear Lord, where I first
believed.

I open my eyes; the song is actually playing on my tape. I get pen and paper and begin to write:

Dear Social Worker,

You have gone on with your life, unaware of the damage you have caused in mine. So many times as a teenager, I wished that I could talk to someone like you to let you know about my pain and suffering.

Please understand you were right in terms of my physical needs being met. As you know we had a grocery store and I was fed beyond my needs. I wore the best of clothes, and lived in a home that was immaculately clean and well kept.

Social Worker, you missed the most important element of my need and that was love. Oh! My adopted dad Eleazer loved me to the core of his heart. His unconditional love for me drew me involuntarily into conflict with my adoptive mother Vi. You see, Social Worker, you only checked the exterior conditions of that family. Had you investigated further you would have found the toxic dynamics that forever impacted my life.

I have been angry with you for years because you placed me in that home and for the times you came to see me, you didn't see me. You talked to Vi but I was invisible to you even though I was in the same room. Had you looked closely you would have seen my fear, my hurt and my pain, but you chose not to. I was invisible to you and you became invisible to me. I cannot put a face to your presence and for a long time I denied your existence in my life.

You placed me in a family that had an existing circle of abuse. My grandmother (Vi's mother) and Vi had some serious issues that were never resolved. They both died never acknowledging or sorting out their problems. I had a grandmother who doted on me and loved me, but held her daughter in high contempt. I had a mother who detested her mother and used me as her "batter girl" for her anger. None of us deserved the abuse bestowed on us, but no one came to rescue and help us. Social Worker, you were a major part of my abuse. You placed me in that cycle.

What I need to tell you, Social Worker, is that Vi was not a bad woman. If she had gotten the help she needed before adopting me she would have been a wonderful mother. She did the best she could with what she had. You gave her the biggest challenge of her life. I believe in her own way she loved me but could not give me love because she did not know love. Her inner battle was not being loved, acknowledged and validated by her mother. Sadly, this was her "Right of Passage" to me.

In my heart of heart, Social Worker, I don't believe Vi ever meant to hurt me. I do believe in her times of anger she was not able to help herself. I believe also there were times her pain became so deep she needed to empty, and I became her personal trash bin. You, Social Worker, placed me in that vulnerable position. Sadly, I don't feel I am alone. I wonder how many other people have been placed by the system and became invisible. I know your argument will be what about the good placements. You will probably list me as one of your successes. But I want you to note this; those that share a similar experience like mine live with a lifetime of damage. No message of success can remove any of that pain.

My final word to you, Social Worker, is that I have survived. I will continue to use my experience to help others. I will use it as well to enlighten your peers about the "invisible children" that fall through the cracks of the system. I will demonstrate the devastation and destruction of our lives. I will solicit their attention and incite change.

Lastly, I forgive you Social Worker, and that has not been an easy task!

Yours Sincerely,
Phyllis Marsh-Jarvis

I Am Now Visible

The music on my tape is right on time. As I sing to the tune "I Just Can't Give Up Now," I am singing to my social worker:

> *I just can't give up now*
> *I've come too far from where I started from*
> *No one told me the road would be easy*
> *But I don't believe He brought me to this far to leave me*

I sing the chorus louder and louder:

> *I just can't give up now,*
> *I've come too far from where I started from*

The song is right. I can't give up now. This has to be my last torturous Mother's Day. There's one more letter to write. There are things I need to say. For years I allowed my freedom to take charge of me; I allowed it to colour my world dark. No more. I choose to become visible.

Being Visible and Being Empowered

Dear Mommy,

It's been a long, long time since you and I spoke. Our last conversation was upsetting because you were leaving me for good but I didn't know it. I knew you were not well that day. When we spoke on the phone and you told me to come I thought we would talk when I got home. I was coming home to take care of you like I always did.

Daddy took me aside one day and made me promise to take care of you. He told me not to hold the things you did to me against you. Mommy, he loved you unconditionally and worried about you. I realize he knew you needed help but he didn't know how to help you. Somehow, Mommy, I also think he knew your story and at some point in your lives he made a commitment to himself he would never turn his back on you no matter what the cost. I became that cost, Mommy. I want you to know even without the promise to him that I would have taken care you. I loved you, Mommy.

I want to tell you that your actions were a high price for me to pay. It's okay, though, because if any of the blows you hammered on me gave you some peace of mind or some comfort then my pain was worth it. You see, Mommy, I loved you with all of my heart. All I ever wanted was your love and your approval. All I wanted was to hear you say the words "I love you." All I ever wanted was a hug. All I ever wanted was to hear you say you were proud of me. I realize now you were not able to give me any of this because it was never given to you. It's okay, Mommy. You and I are all right.

I apologize, if Daddy loving me and doting on me made you feel badly. I know that he was the only one who loved you and I think when I came along you felt threatened and jealous. I also understand that the love Granny showed for me, the friendship that she and I shared, should have been yours. Granny was tough on you as a mother when I was growing up with you. You didn't deserve her scorn no matter what mistakes you may have made. You and she seemed to hate each other. The older I got I couldn't understand the disrespectful relationship you and she had.

Do you remember the day I scolded you about paying so much attention to an older woman in our community and you ignoring Granny? You acted as though this woman was your mother. It made me feel sorry for my grandmother. You made me take food to this other lady and you wouldn't do anything for Granny. It was confusing and hurtful to me, so I told you I refused to recognize this lady and ignore my grandmother.

How could you expect me to respect you when you didn't respect your mother? I did, but it was damn hard. You didn't say anything to me that day. You could have explained to me about you and Granny but you didn't. The saddest thing for me is that both you and Granny left this earth without making peace with each other.

I didn't want that to happen to us, Mommy. On your final day I wanted to let you know how much I loved you, but you left before I got the chance. If I had only gotten home on time we could have had a long talk. I would have said all the things Granny didn't say and that you needed to hear. I would have told you how much you meant to me all these years even though I was afraid of you. I would have told you how proud I was of you, especially when you went out of your way to help others, never looking for anything in return. I would have thanked you for making me the responsible woman I am.

Mommy, I would have held you in my arms and comforted you in your pain. I would have wiped the tears from your eyes; I would have kissed you on your cheek and your forehead. I would not have left your side, until you were ready for your final sleep.

Mommy, I am sorry I was not there. Please forgive me. I have had a hard time forgiving myself.

I was devastated when you left me. I felt so alone. I'll share a secret with you. You know how close Daddy and I were. Well, when you left me I took losing you harder than I did losing him. I never thought that was possible! My life was so off balance after you left. I struggled to survive. I became emotionally sick and lived in total denial. In my younger years when you were still alive I confused sex with love, drank excessively and was extremely angry. After you left, these things became much worse.

I have had struggles, Mommy, with my emotions for about twenty-three years and like you I hurt the people closest to me along the way. I've lost them, Mommy. I have suffered the biggest losses of my life because of my cycle of baggage, perhaps justifiably so. Mommy, perhaps like you, lost in my void I have made some horrific mistakes.

I wish you were here so we could talk. There are days when all I want to do is bare my soul to you and have you hold me close to your heart and tell me everything is going to be okay. You see, we have something in common: all we both ever wanted was our mother's love. We both allowed our void to dictate who we had become and not who we really were. Unfortunately, no one acknowledged our pain. We both were invisible.

Mommy, my favourite hymn is playing . . .

> *Through it all, through it all*
> *I learned to trust in Jesus, I learned to trust in God*
> *Through it all . . .*

Mommy, these hymns soothe my spirit, especially on days like this. God is the centre of my life and that's how I have been able to forgive myself and forgive all my abusers.

You know, Mommy, it just wasn't you; I was sexually abused by two men and a woman in our community. They all said the same thing to me, that if I told you they would say I was lying and you would beat me. I never told you because I was afraid. Mommy, they used you against me and I let them. I wouldn't tell Daddy because I knew he would tell you. I knew you would beat me and he wouldn't do anything to help me. While that was going on I hated you and I blamed you for what was happening to me. I truly felt it was your fault. Please forgive me.

Did you know that after you beat me and left me in my room, I would crawl on my bed in the fetal position and pray and make promises to God that if he would let me meet my real mother I would be good?

I did get to meet her, Mommy; she was so different from you. You were tall and firm and stoic in stature, while she was short and wonderfully chubby. She was gentle in spirit and soft-spoken, unlike you who exuded dominance and strictness.

Your skin was the most rich, velvety chocolate brown. I remember the closest I got to you, as a little girl, was when you were dressing and I would rub my little hands along your naked back as we sat on the bed and you would let me. Your skin was like satin. I have never forgotten that. It was one of the most wonderful feelings of my life and I have always wanted to get that feeling back. Leah Jarvis, my biological mother, had skin that was a tinge away from white; it too was soft and smooth. You were both so different, and I believe I mirror both of you.

Ironically, Mommy, she too was set aside by "the system." Can you imagine that she was institutionalized and then lost in the system for years, that her family had no idea where she was? One day my Cousin Ruth (deceased) received a call from a nursing home in Meteghan. When the family went, there was Mom with matted hair, very unkempt. It appears that no one could tell the family where she was. Is that not bizarre? Like us, she had become invisible within "the system."

Mommy, I had five wonderful years with her. Somehow, though, I felt the joy we shared was a double-edged sword for her. As much as she was happy with the time we shared, often I could see from her facial expression that I was a reminder of her burdens from the past. Her long deep sighs confirmed my hidden thoughts. I wish you two had met. Eventually I think you may have become good friends. I think you both could have bared your souls to each other.

Mommy, what I need to share with you about meeting my real mother is that I loved her from the moment I saw her. She was everything I thought she would be.

But you know what didn't change, which I did not want to admit all these years? What didn't change was the fact that you were my mother. No matter what you and I had been through, you were the person who raised me. As much as I tried to sever the connection between you and me, by meeting my biological mother, that invisible umbilical cord could not be broken. Throughout our tyranny there was a definite bond. Mommy, did you feel that bond?

Mommy, I was angry with God for a long time. I just could not understand why he put me through this. I have learned we all have a purpose in this life on earth. I have taken my scars and turned them into teachable moments. Mommy, I champion a cause for you, my biological mother Leah and me.

I talk to people, Mommy, giving them my testimony, not to say you were bad, but to give a voice to those of us who became invisible to the system. I reach out to the social workers to be more diligent in the lives of children who will be impacted for life by their one decision. I try to encourage women who have been invisible to become visible by getting help.

Also, by sharing our story I hope to create awareness they are not alone. Mommy, I hope through the experience of the three of us – you, Leah and me – other people will share their stories. Mommy, we need to advocate continuously for change within the "social service system." Thank you, Mommy, for giving me the courage to speak out. Whenever I speak I take you with me in my heart.

Mommy, I have so much more to say, but I have a feeling you and I will talk more. Please come into my dreams; I long to see you. I love you, Mommy. Happy blessed Mother's Day. Rest in peace, you and I are all right. I love you from the depths of my heart, Mommy. I have always loved you even when I felt hatred for you. Forgive me, Mommy!

Your loving daughter
Phyllis

This has been an emotionally difficult day. It has been a day to rejoice and a day to reflect deeply into the past. Going back and facing my ghosts has given me the freedom to celebrate my two mothers. We are free and we are visible.

Happy Mother's Day, Leah and Violet. I love you both unconditionally. Thank you, God, for the two beautiful gifts you bestowed on me: my two mothers. Happy blessed Mother's Day to you both!

Dedicated to my two mothers
Leah Jarvis – biological mother
Violet Muriel Marsh – adopted mother
Humbly shared by their daughter
Phyllis Marsh-Jarvis

Healing – At Last I Am Visible

Ah! Here I am, blessed to be at the age of fifty-seven years. I have risen from the depths of despair: physical abuse, emotional abuse, and years of being burdened with a broken spirit. My healing was not a Band-aid fix for me with a few visits to a therapist. No, I had to face the damage of a torn soul and peel off the layers of anger, hatred and hurt. This was a lonely and troubled process. Revisiting all that had been done to me and finding forgiveness within my heart was grueling and scary work. The most challenging part of this process was taking responsibility for my actions and behaviour. Accepting that I was not responsible for what had been done to me but that I was responsible for my actions was a hard pill to swallow. You see, I felt she had made me the way that I was and it was her fault and the social worker's fault and all those people around me who couldn't save me – it was their fault.

I spent a great portion of my life wanting to give back the pain that was placed on me. When I was unsuccessful I wanted to hurt myself and I could only do that through self-pity, heavy drinking, thoughts of suicide, playing the victim, and using low self-esteem as my crutch. My saving grace was God's mercy. My experience of abuse has become my gift. My gift is now my ministry. I have become visible through my voice. Had I not gone through what I did I could not minister hope and survival to other victims. I would not be able to let social workers know the actual pain and suffering we go through because of some of their decisions. I have risen and changed my scars into stars. I am visible and I hope that social workers who read my story will find it helpful as they make life-changing decisions and recommendations about the lives of vulnerable children. As I returned to university to pursue higher education, I initially considered the social work field, but who knows where this journey will lead me.

An excerpt from "Footprints in the Sand" comforts me:

. . . The Lord replied, *"My precious, precious child,*
I love you and I would never leave you,
During your times of trial and suffering when
You see only one set of footprints in the sand, it was then that I
carried you."

He did from the time I was a little girl and He continues to carry me to this day. I am truly blessed. I have found my joy in the gifts He gave me my voice, my testimonies.

I have risen
I have risen beyond the years of fears
I have risen despite the heartfelt tears
I do not rise nor stand alone
I rise for my mothers in their eternal home
Forever I will be their voice
Singing hope and chanting the truth of choice
Their journey of hope, my sisters abused; let us rejoice
And tell the world we found our voice
I have risen

Section Four:

Making Institutional Change

Chapter 15

Africentric Perspectives In Social Work: Views From Nova Scotia

Wanda Thomas Bernard, Winnie Benton, Rene Baptiste

Introduction (Wanda Thomas Bernard)

Research is the production of knowledge about a given subject and the people who produce such knowledge increase their ability to deal with the particular issues involved (Bernard 1996). We contend that if ordinary people are engaged in research as active agents of the experience, we essentially help them to enhance their capacity to effect change in their conditions. Returning to Halifax in 1995, after spending two years in Sheffield, England, doing doctoral work, I was keen to share my interest in Africentric theory with other African Nova Scotians. However, most of the available literature was American-based, and located in the fields of education or psychology. I was interested in the application of Africentric theory in social work practice and education in Canada.

This was a work in progress, further development of my interest in Black Perspectives in social work, but I believed that this should be a collective process. (We use the term Black and African Nova Scotian interchangeably in this report.) Hence the research project was designed to involve other African Nova Scotians in a study about our experiences in social work education and practice. Connecting the personal and political agenda, this research is part of that journey, and our collective struggle to bring African centred perspectives from the margins to the mainstream.

The research for *Africentric Perspectives in Social Work: Views From Nova Scotia* was funded by the Multicultural Program of the Department of Canadian Heritage, and jointly sponsored by the Maritime School of Social Work (MSSW) and the Association of Black Social Workers (ABSW). It was conducted from 1996 to 1998.

In an attempt to theorize about Africentricity and social work practice, I began with the following principles of Africentric perspectives (Bernard 1996):

1. The recognition of a distinct African and Africentric world view;

2. The development of African centredness and an acknowledgement of our shared experiences of racism, colonialism and imperialism and the impact of these;

3. Knowledge of African history, and the location and relocation of Africans on the Continent and throughout the Diaspora;

4. The promotion of African cultural elements, traditions and practices;

5. Empowerment and liberation as central to practice.

This framework underpins my teaching, research, practice and my life. It is the integration of these in all aspects of my work and my life that have helped to move me from a position of powerlessness to being empowered to critique existing paradigms, to create new ones, and to serve not only African people, but all people more effectively.

We began the research with a review of the relevant literature on Africentricity.

Africentricity

Africentricity is defined by Asante as the belief in the centrality of Africans in postmodern history. It is our own history, our mythology, our creative motif and ethos exemplifying our collective will (1988, p. 6). The theory and the practice of Africentricity places African people at the centre of social and historical experiences, rather than peripheral to European ones. It is concerned with African people as subjects of those experiences, rather than objects. Asante (1988) states that Africentricity seeks to change the way we refer to ourselves and our experiences, past and present, incorporating innovation as well as tradition.

A central theme of Africentricity is the creation of a new African methodology that allows Africans to control knowledge about themselves. Africentric theorists have created the theory of Africology, which is defined as the Africentric study of phenomena, events, ideas, and personalities related to Africa and Africans in the Diaspora.

The key features of Africentricity are: oneness of being, notion of interdependence, being in harmony with nature, the nature of being as spirit, harmonious fusion, and synthesis between people and their reality (Asante 1988). Africentric theory is a theory of affirmation, conceived to generate new knowledge and to pursue the path of liberation (Bekerie 1994, p. 133). In assessing Africentricity and its implications for higher education, Schiele (1994a) does a comparative analysis of Africentric and Eurocentric views of people. These are outlined below in Diagram One.

DIAGRAM ONE

AFRICENTRIC WORLD VIEW	EUROCENTRIC WORLD VIEW
Emphasis on harmony and collectivity	Emphasis on domination, conflict and fragmentation
Collective and non-materialistic orientation towards people	Individualistic and materialistic orientation towards life
Emphasis on non-material or intangible qualities of people	Emphasis on material and physical attributes of people
More holistic conception of people from a collective and spiritual perspective	Emphasis on individual differences
Emphasis on discerning similarities or commonalties of people	More restricted, fragmented and individualistic conception of people

These divergent views are imbedded in the different world views, and reflected in different ways of experiencing, knowing and expressing reality. The Africentric world view offers a more holistic conception of human beings (Schiele 1994b, p. 154). One objective of Africentric science is human liberation (Akbar 1984); consequently, this theory has relevance for all of humanity. "[Africentricity] is both specific and universal: it speaks to the specific liberation needs of people of African descent and to the spiritual and moral development of the world" (Schiele 1996, p. 286).

Using the same principles of Africentricity, Karenga (1978) developed the Africentric value system. The goals of Karenga's value system, named **Nguzo Saba**, are to help African people work together and to respect themselves and each other; and to promote and celebrate our collective history, identity and struggle. There are seven principles of Nguzo Saba:

Umoja (unity) – strive for and maintain unity in the family, community, nation and race;

Kujichaguila (self-determination) – to define ourselves, name ourselves, create for ourselves and speak for ourselves;

Ujima (collective work and responsibility) – to build and maintain community together; to make sisters' and brothers' problems our problems, and to solve them together;

Ujamma (cooperative economics) – to build and maintain our own shops, stores, businesses, and to profit from these together;

Nia (purpose) – to make our collective vocation the building and development of our community in order to restore our people to traditional greatness;

Kuumba (creativity) – to do all we can to leave our community more beautiful and beneficial than we inherited it;

Imani (faith) – to believe in our people, our parents, our teachers, our leaders and the righteousness and victory of our struggles.

These principles are considered the foundation for African families and communities.

Collins (1990, p. 27) argues that the continuation of an Africentric world view has been fundamental to African-Americans' resistance to racial oppression. We offer similar comment regarding the resistance and survival of African Nova Scotians. Furthermore, Collins (1990) says that the key dimensions of an Africentric feminist standpoint are: concrete experiences are a criterion of meaning; dialogue is used in assessing knowledge claims; and it encompasses the ethics of caring and accountability. Jerome Schiele's (1996, p. 286) view concurs with Collins' perspective:

1) human identity is a collective identity;

2) the spiritual or non-material component of human beings is just as important and valid as the material component; and

3) the affective approach to knowledge is epistemologically valid. (Affective epistemology is the individual's experience.)

This research was informed by an Africentric perspective: that is, using a world view that sees African people as critical agents of their own experience. The core focus of the Africentric paradigm is the reassessment of social phenomena from an African-centred orientation (Schiele 1996, Asante 1987, Collins 1990). Africentric theory as espoused here is the theoretical base used to construct accounts of social work practice as described by social workers and human service workers of African descent, practising in Nova Scotia.

The Practical Application of Africentric Theory

Premises of Africentric Research Methods

Africentric research is holistic, integrative, and participatory. The main objective of our project was not to produce knowledge about the African Nova Scotian practitioners but rather to engage African Nova Scotian practitioners in a dialogue about their experience. This was an opportunity for practitioners to name their experience and, furthermore, to describe and analyze that experience.

Research Methods Used in This Study

Data was collected in two phases. In phase one, African social workers and human service workers completed a mailed survey. From a list of ninety workers throughout Nova Scotia, fifty completed questionnaires were returned. A thematic analysis was used to identify the main themes emerging from the questionnaire data.

In phase two of the research we held focus groups in central locations throughout the province, as another means of data gathering, thereby achieving data triangulation. In addition, this was a means of extending our preliminary analysis of the data gathered via the questionnaire, building in member checks to enhance data trustworthiness. The themes were used to guide the focus group discussions. A thematic analysis was also used to analyze the focus group data.

Challenges

Like any new theory, particularly one that challenges traditional paradigms, Africentrism has been the subject of much criticism and debate. We believe this is good, in many respects, as it forces us to clearly articulate the Africentric paradigm and engages scholars in critical research, which tests its effectiveness.

Some recent debates challenge Africentricity's lack of attention to class and privilege or differences in social status and material realities in African communities. Others argue that Africentricity offers no substance to bring about systemic change in the world. Some Africentrists posit that systemic racism in higher education seeks to maintain the hegemony of Eurocentrism; therefore, it will not or cannot allow for the development of Africentric ideas.

Still others argue that "Africentricity" is rhetoric espoused by Asante that does not have a sound theoretical base. If you asked twenty African Nova Scotians to define Africentrism, you are likely to get twenty different responses. This is good, because it suggests that Africans can be agents of their own experience and their own spokespersons and liberations.

The analysis of the data is constructed from a framework that the Africentric discourse identifies as the Interpretation/Analysis component of Africentric methodology. An Africentric orientation, concerned with establishing a world view about the writing and speaking of oppressed people, challenges the assumptions of Eurocentric research about the African experience. As Jerome Schiele (1996) states, an Africentric orientation provides both a more accurate and informative view of the African experience, and contributes to a more accurate and informative understanding of the diversity of human experiences.

Challenging Eurocentric ideology about the charges made against the African experience, which are mainly constructed from assumption and not from first voice experience, is considered to be radical; however, Africentric orientation sees this challenge as necessary and argues that: To create a radical assessment of a given reality is to create, among other things, another reality (Asante, 1987, p. 5).

From this discussion, the questions then become: "What is the reality of the practitioners of African descent practising social work in Nova Scotia?" and "What components of their reality support an Africentric perspective?" The results from phase one of the research are reported next.

Practitioners' Responses

As noted above, phase one of the research was conducted by questionnaire format, with thirteen questions examining areas such as educational achievement, career development, and frameworks of practice. Questions one and two examined respondents' educational achievement. Of the fifty responses received the majority of practitioners had their Bachelor's Degree, 20% had their Master's Degree and 20% had certificates or diplomas. Only two of the fifty respondents were supervisors, with one of the two working in the field of social work.

For the majority of the participants, the current job was the second or third social work position. Some participants had seven or eight positions in social work prior to the current position. Forty participants were in full-time positions; however, twenty of these were in government-funded projects that were not permanent; four were in part-time permanent positions; six were in term, or contract positions.

The majority of the participants had more experience in indirect social work, thirty-three of fifty, whereas seventeen of fifty had more years in direct social work, with the maximum being fifteen years. These findings suggest that although the majority of the respondents were qualified at the Diploma or Bachelor's level, most were not employed in permanent positions. There are few

African social workers or human service workers in management positions, and many are employed in indirect social work roles.

When respondents were asked what they believed had the greatest influence on their interaction with their clients, many indicated that it was their life experiences, more specifically, life experiences that were affected by racism. Table One highlights the responses that we elicited from the respondents.

TABLE ONE

INFLUENCES ON PRACTICE	
Your life experiences	42/84%
Your practical experiences	37/74%
Your skill inventory	34/68%
Your education	18/36%
Your theoretical perspective	15/30%

While education and theoretical perspective were seen by the respondents to be components of their practice, they were not seen as being as important as their life experiences, practical experiences, or their skill inventory. The majority of the participants indicated that their life experiences and practical experiences were the greatest influences on their current practice. The following quotations illustrate some of their views:

"My life experiences have made me who I am. Education (university learning) is just one part of my being . . . experiences make people."

". . . Life experiences with poverty, racism and sexism and the skills I've acquired have helped me understand the feelings and emotions of others far more than any theories learned at the Maritime School of Social Work."

Finally, a number of participants indicated that all of the items listed had an influence. One person stated: *"All of the above. I believe all of these are of equal importance and should be combined in every [social] worker's personal praxis."*

While African social workers and human service workers who participated in this study indicate that their life experiences and practical experiences have a significant impact on their practice, they also suggest that this is combined with their education and training to help make them effective practitioners.

When providing a service to an individual client, which brings about change in that individual's life, many respondents felt that they had changed the individual, the community at large, and the individual's family. The responses to this question indicate a collective consciousness and holistic view of society, which is a key component of Africentrism. This is consistent with what the literature says about Africentricity and the validity of affective knowledge. A similar theme emerges when practitioners reflected on the impact of their work with clients. The following quotations reflect participants' opinions regarding the effects of change:

"Change is universal. It is like a pebble in a pool of water. The circle gets larger and larger and in our work you do not just touch that person."

"Any impact on an individual ultimately impacts a broader sphere. . ."

"When you [work] **with** *clients to make positive choices/changes in their lives, their immediate family may also be affected in a positive way . . . [H]owever, world and community change goes beyond the individual. We must work as allies to restructure policies and practices before change can occur on such levels . . ."*

Africentric scholars state that a knowledge of our shared history and an analysis of racism and its daily effects are the underpinnings of an Africentric consciousness (Essed 1991, Collins 1990, Asante 1999). Questions around the relevance of race were asked to elicit participants' perspectives on this issue. When respondents were asked if their race was relevant in providing a service, ninety percent responded yes, as can be seen in Table Two below.

TABLE TWO

RELEVANCE OF RESPONDENTS' RACE	
Yes	45/90%
No	3/6%
Yes/No	1/2%
No response	1/2%

One participant emphasized the shared history and experience of racial oppression:

"Yes, I do believe that my race is relevant when providing a service. I believe that I can relate to clients of African descent on a level that a white social worker cannot because I can identify with the client culturally. I may be more aware of and sensitive to issues that are affecting the client, as well as understanding the barriers they may have to cope with."

Other respondents, who also answered yes, talked about systemic racism that is imbedded in institutions:

"Yes, most definitely. In the rural Black communities residents have no access to Black social workers, teachers, lawyers, etc. Those individuals employed by the local agencies are not sensitive to the needs/issues that face the Black communities or other marginalized groups. The services received by most Black clients are inadequate and discriminatory at the very least. My intervention has ensured that those clients that I assist receive the same services or benefits enjoyed by the mainstream community."

Those who responded that their race was not relevant, six percent, did recognize that it might be a factor. For example, one person stated no because they felt that *"if you are experienced and well trained in dealing with the issues that affect your client's needs, your race may not be totally relevant."*

When asked if they felt that their client's race is relevant when providing a service, seventy percent responded yes. A number of

196

participants responded yes and no, which exemplifies the complexity of the issue.

TABLE THREE

RELEVANCE OF CLIENTS' RACE	
Yes	35/70%
No	6/12%
Yes/No	8/16%
No Response	1/2%

The following quotations help to illuminate this complexity and the *yes* and *no* responses:

"Yes, some clients in the Black community express their concerns, and gratitude in having an African Nova Scotian in the community, working, helping with their problems, providing services, information, showing concern for the client and their families, understanding their background and culture and not feeling inferior. No, when providing services for clients who are not African Nova Scotians, race is not relevant to me because their problems and concerns are just the same as other clients. Regardless of who they are, I would do my best to help them and provide the best service possible for both African Nova Scotians and others because I see my clients as people who need help and understanding and would like to provide that without prejudice."

These views suggest that race may be more relevant for African Nova Scotian clients, who are not accustomed to being served by a practitioner of their race. Racial matching might break down some of the barriers that are inherent in the helping relationship. However, for non-African clients, the emphasis is more on providing quality service, regardless of race. Yet, as previously noted, the workers' experience of racial oppression helps them to understand other types of oppression, enabling them to use their experiences when helping clients.

Most respondents articulated that their client's race was relevant, particularly when the client was from a marginalized group. The following response illuminates this view:

"Absolutely! It [race] frames their reality in this racist . . . society. I work with the client's race, and experiences of racism in the context of helping to raise their consciousness about their . . . situation."

Those who responded no, their client's race was not relevant, emphasized their willingness and ability to work with clients regardless of their race.

"Although I believe my race is relevant when providing service to a client, I do not think the client's race is relevant . . . In my years of practice I have always assessed and assisted clients on their true needs . . . regardless of race."

As evidenced in the participants' voices presented above, race and racism do matter in their practice. The findings suggest that African Nova Scotian social workers and human service workers are painfully aware of racism, and how this impacts on their practice with African and non-African clients. Furthermore, they suggest that their awareness and analysis of racism can be a strength and resource in their work, as it helps them to understand other forms of oppression that their clients likely experience. Essentially, participants see their location as African people who are marginalized by their race, as a unique experience that helps to frame and contextualize their practice.

When asked about this, ninety-two percent of the respondents felt that there were unique qualities and values that direct their practice. The following qualities were identified: learned survival strategies around identifying and dealing with racism, cultural identity, and collective consciousness. The following examples highlight the qualities that participants identified:

"My belief and value of our [African] heritage, strength, endurance and desire for our people to succeed."

"I view every case as an opportunity to change the way in which society sees the African male. My very presence is an indication that … we too are affected by the social forces and are able to show compassion for those who are most affected."

These responses are linked to the notion of collective consciousness and the significance not only of one's life experiences, but the interpretation of those experiences.

Those who answered no stated that all social workers are unique, and therefore bring distinct qualities to their work. This view emphasizes the issue of humanity and how that influences one's view of the world.

Clearly, the majority of our respondents do believe that they bring unique qualities to their work, and this appears to be linked to their everyday experience of racism and the survival strategies that they have employed. The greatest emphasis seems to be on how they use their experiences to help others who may be dealing with different, but similar struggles.

The final set of questions were asked to elicit participants' views on service provision in the African Nova Scotian community. Ninety percent of the respondents indicated that they did not feel that the services provided to the African Nova Scotian community were adequate. When answering no, most respondents indicated inadequacies in the areas of poor fostering and adoption services; poor representation of Black workers in agencies; lack of parent support programs for clients; lack of drug therapy programs; no mentoring; and a lack of training and education around issues that affect the African client.

An overwhelming majority believes that there is a lack of services available to African Nova Scotian clients, and both rural and urban workers share these views. Those who answered yes, saying they felt the services were adequate, qualified their answers with such responses as the following:

"I do believe that the services provided the African Nova Scotian community are indeed adequate; however, they need to be further developed

and expanded. Some services are designed to keep us in the dependency mode. Somehow we must break the cycle."

"Adequate yes, effective no."

"The services provided only scratch the surface of the needs of African Nova Scotian youth and community at large..."

The analysis presented here is clear. African Nova Scotian social workers and human service workers overwhelmingly agree that service provision is inadequate. They are particularly concerned about the lack of culturally relevant services for African clients.

Conclusion

The questionnaire results indicate that there is an integration of the tenets of Africentric theory evident in the practice of social workers and human service workers of African descent in Nova Scotia. Participants' awareness of the impact of racism, the cultural connectedness, collective consciousness, the significance of affective knowledge, and the holistic perspective of practice are all indicators of engagement with Africentric theoretical principles. These were further explored in the regional focus groups.

Three major themes emerged from our data analysis: that life experiences are significant to the practice of social work for African Nova Scotian workers; that they operate with a sense of collective consciousness; and finally, current services were not adequate to meet the needs of African Nova Scotian clients. Therefore, the focus group questions sought clarification of items one and two, and recommendations for change, to address item three.

Focus Groups Results

Life Experiences

From the interviews we learned that African Nova Scotian social workers and human service workers relied more on their life experiences to guide their practice with clients. This is consistent with

Africentric theory, which argues that affective epistemology, authenticity, creativity, cultural awareness and self-determination are key principles of African philosophy, which guides theory and practice.

Through the focus groups the participants provided more detailed information regarding how they felt their life experiences guided their practice with their clients. A common theme that emerged in each of the focus groups was the sharing of similar life experiences with clients, as is reflected in this response: *". . . experience is also based on skills that you might have learned over time, so you try to pass those skills on or try to show them how you got those skills through experience."*

This concept speaks to one of the key principals of the African philosophy, which is that affective epistemology – the individual's experience – is a valid way of knowing and is worth sharing with others. As one participant aptly states, *"I think that's a very powerful place to start and bring people into their own sense of empowerment and their own sense of understanding that who they are and what their experiences are about is not invalid, but valid."*

Another participant stressed the value of linking education with life experiences. Either would be insufficient on its own, but the collective helps to make the individual worker more effective in practice: *". . . [I]t's almost like a part-in-parcel me; without the life experiences I don't think the education would've been it. You need them both. It just kind of ties in all together, but that's the connectors. To me it's kind of like you live and breathe it. I get excited when I think about at some point going off and doing some more formal education, because it's the learning. I always want to know what else is there to learn . . . and how that fits with what I already know . . ."*

Respondents felt that if they had a sense of who they were and how they were shaped by their life experiences then they could provide better service to their clients. For example, one person stated that: *"If you know what your own perspective is and what your life experiences bring to your practice, well then, I think you're able to work with a variety of different people from other communities as well."*

This knowledge of self is seen as a way to allow African practitioners to connect with the client through shared experiences.

Life experiences are seen by the practitioners as providing a method to make the connection between the collective and the spiritual component of their clients. One person said: *"[W]hen I look at these life experiences of people from an Africentric perspective, I look at the traditions and the lessons that were passed on to me by my elders. And sort of like religion, but your morals were always engrained in you, it was a long arduous journey."*

This connection with spirituality is consistent with Jerome Schiele's (2000) perspective on the role of spirituality in Africentric social work. This participant added, *"[L]ife experience has to become internalized and it becomes part of what you use to either set your own judgements, your own set of values, your own set of beliefs. So I think there's something to how our life experience helps get you to be more grounded in something, because you not only experienced it but you now can make an assumption about what somebody else is like . . .*

Spirituality is seen as a source of strength, particularly if it is part of a collective and communal involvement. Schiele (1996) asserts that a spiritual force is present in all things and there is a spiritual connection between people and nature. For many people experiencing social problems, there is a disconnection or spiritual alienation. Therefore, a goal in social work intervention would be reconnection. Participants of the focus groups indicated that social work is about knowing and connecting, which are key components of Africentricity. One participant sums it up nicely: *". . . knowing and connecting not only with my sense of personhood, but it connects with my sense of identity that I am located not only within my family, but within my community."*

Theorizing through shared experience, and being able to theorize from that space is a form of resistance and survival for Africans in the Diaspora (Bernard 1996, Collins 1990, Schiele 1996). That sense of knowing and connecting through life experiences also links to the principal of collective consciousness.

Collective Consciousness

We asked participants in the focus groups to describe collective consciousness. We began with the basic premise that a sense of interconnectedness, rootedness and unity are key to Africentric theory and practice. Participants informed us that there definitely is a sense of collective consciousness within their work and daily lives.

As one participant shares: *"To me collective consciousness is the fact that because of who we are, we are conscious of what's out there that we have to face together, or individually. But we have to work towards change so that we can achieve together."*

This awareness of collective consciousness has both a community local component and connection to the larger Diaspora, as evidenced by the comments below.

"When I think back to when I was a kid, the community was everything. Everybody was concerned about everybody and everything that went on in the community. It didn't just affect your family, it affected everybody's family and a connectedness to the larger Diaspora."

Another participant said: *"And once or twice I've had to walk through the whole aisle of people and my eyes will only connect with somebody who is of the same colour as me and they'll give me acknowledgement."*

Collective consciousness was seen by the respondents to be inclusive and holistic. Participants reflected on the unconscious decisions and acts that are rooted in a keen awareness of our collective experiences and challenges. One person, referring to the experience of racism in the workplace, indicated that collective consciousness was knowing that you had support: *"[W]e're defending each other and supporting each other."*

[Collective consciousness is] *"...based upon norms and values, personal life experience and perspectives. It's about inclusivity, not exclusivity. It's about kids, as well as elders, as well as adults being part of a process. Collective consciousness is about responsibility."*

Participants also referred to the ways in which collective consciousness influenced their practice in social work. One participant stated: *". . . we have a responsibility to the well-being, emotional, physical and spiritual building of each other and ourselves. And when we do that there's a consciousness about that. And sometimes it's unconscious; sometimes we don't even think about it but I think that's just part of our acculturation. And a collective consciousness means that we all have the same starting point but it doesn't mean we're always at the same ending point. We're on a continual, constant learning and we share that learning."*

Another participant stated that it allowed them to connect with their clients in a unique way: *"With me for work, I'll see people come in and . . . I'll see the Black people come in, and it's almost like I know what they're going through. And it's like this feeling, like you . . . have that collective feeling toward that person. You know they have needs and you know that as soon as they leave the door then they're ready to go for an interview. You know darn well, they're probably going to get the door slammed in their face, so there is that collectiveness there that makes deep emotions, and the hurt is in there . . . you can see it in their faces . . ."*

There is also a shared experience between worker and client that often goes unspoken but is acknowledged in other ways or at a later time, as noted during one focus group session: *"I'm thinking of the consciousness and as an example related to what I do in employment, often times clients will come in for counselling and usually before that step to employment (there's a variety of steps that you take to prepare someone for employment) there's always a collective consciousness with regard to how you as a Black person will respond and react in certain circumstances."*

However, for some African Nova Scotian workers this can represent higher expectations and unmet needs. One person stated: *"On the other side of that too I find clients have very high expectations of you as the practitioner because they think you should know and you should connect with them in a different way than just anybody else. And I find that they can be very easily disappointed. So I find what has to happen is that you have to be very honest and clear in working with Black clients, and that's just been part of my experience in learn-ing that. And I had to learn that because you want to be so helpful and you want the person to think yeah, and you did come to the right person and yeah, I am here to help you. But then you leave the person with the impression that you can move mountains and you can't move mountains, you can only do what you can do. So I think you have to be really cautious and conscious of that as well."*

Another participant said that by ensuring that our work was positive and relevant, then collectively we could help to facilitate change. Respondents clearly appeared to recognize that their indi-vidual and collective identity was influenced by and influenced their experiences and their practice in their communities.

One participant articulates this point clearly: *"This question of collective consciousness came up earlier in the day . . . I think that it's an identification that you see yourself belonging to a group. As well, not only is there an identification, but there's an internalized aware-ness that identifies automatically that there's something that you can connect to with somebody else as we perceive the world and how it operates according to colour, according to language. So a collective consciousness to me speaks to that identity – that is, you are consciously aware . . ."*

At times that conscious awareness is a central part of resistance and survival. Participants addressed the sharing of positive strate-gies to survive and the struggles that African people endure and overcome daily: *"There is a collective pain in our community too. And sometimes I think we're mystified by it. And sometimes we're in denial about it. And sometimes it's just right in our face. But there's a collective pain and we share it, just as much as there is a collective joy. You know, we celebrate marriages and we mourn funerals. That's a very powerful thing. There is a very collective pain. I think that as a people sometimes we don't know what to do with our pain and I think that's . . . the reason why there's just the lack of services that are avail-able for us as people of African descent. But also the fact that some-times we don't know where to put our pain and we . . . we internalize it . . . there's a consciousness about that too . . . "*

To conclude, through the focus groups, participants clearly articulated their understandings of the impact and influences of life experiences and collective consciousness on their practice of social work and human service work. The shared experiences of racism, resistance, and resilience informed their work with clients, and their relationships with colleagues. Life experiences underpin the notion of collective consciousness, which is a shared awareness and analysis of history and experiences. Participants share a consciousness of oppression and its effects with their clients, which may enable them to get closer to their clients' truth. Theorizing from that space of collective consciousness, rooted in lived experiences, is akin to seeing Africentricity in action. It is moving from the particular individual experience to the global, collective one, to effect individual and collective change.

Discussions and Recommendations

Africentric theory is about rooting the experiences of Africans in the Diaspora in African culture, history, world view, philosophy and experiences, or the centring of those experiences as a beginning frame of reference for analysis and action. Asante (1999, p. 9) states that after centuries of oppression, many African people have lost their sense of agency, as they have been robbed of their heritage and their identity. Africentric theory is thus a corrective, or reclaiming, of African traditions and a critique of European domination of Africa and African people. The reclaiming of one's African heritage and identity is a challenging process in a non-African environment, and as Benton (1997) notes, people need to be supported on this journey. Social workers and human service workers working from an Africentric orientation are central to that process.

There has been little attention in the literature to the application of Africentric theory in social work practice, yet the principles and philosophy are similar to social justice principles. As a theory of affirmation and liberation, Africentricity allows Africans to control knowledge about themselves and to challenge oppressive structures and practices. Linking the past, present and future, Tukufu (1997) states that Africentric theory is also a celebration of African people's struggle, resistance and survival. Schiele (1996) stresses that Africentricity in social work has three main objectives in practice as it:

seeks to promote an alternative social science paradigm reflective of the cultural and political reality of African Americans;

seeks to dispel negative distortions about African people;

seeks to promote a world view that will facilitate human and social transformation.

Applying this approach in practice, Schiele (1996, p. 289) asserts that the first step is assessing the social inequalities and consequences of social policies on individual problems. Interventions should include approaches that enhance the positive potential of all individuals and the ethic of caring. The helping process is characterized by reciprocity and personalization of the professional relationship. Clients are seen as the experts of their own experiences, and there is a focus on empowerment and social justice for all human beings. Interventions with Africans in the Diaspora would pay particular attention to the historical and current marginalization, colonization and their impact on present problems.

The African Nova Scotian Experience

African Nova Scotian social workers and human service workers who participated in this study expressed an awareness of the impact of racism on them and their clients. They identified a sense of cultural connectedness to their clients and their communities. These workers indicated that affective knowledge is significant in their practice, and that they practise from a holistic perspective. The significance of their life experiences and collective consciousness were two major themes that emerged in the analysis of the data collected from the individual questionnaires. These themes were further explored in the focus groups. There was also an analysis of historical, and current political and structural realities that impact on them as workers and on their clients. Participants also identified a number of gaps in services to African Nova Scotian clients and the lack of culturally appropriate services as a significant concern. These are all indicators of engagement with Africentric theoretical principles.

African Nova Scotian social workers and human service workers share an Africentric world view. Their perspectives on the significance of race, racism, their life experiences and collective consciousness suggest a clear understanding and analysis of the oppression and marginalization of themselves as workers and of their clients. There is recognition of the cultural alienation and disconnection from community that many clients are struggling with. There is also a sense of connection with clients that experience other forms of oppression based on factors such as class, sexual orientation or age. The lived reality of African Nova Scotian workers helps to inform their view of the world and their world view.

While these workers might not have the language of Africentric theory, their discussion and description of their practice are consistent with the theoretical and philosophical underpinnings as outlined above. The lack of engagement with the language might be best explained by the lack of access to the literature. In Canadian Schools of Social Work there has been little attention paid to the Africentric world view. The Dalhousie School of Social Work has only introduced this theory in the curriculum since 1995, and an elective course was developed in 1999, an outcome of this study. As previously noted, there is little attention in the literature on the application of Africentricity in social work. In addition, many of the respondents do not have social work training. The majority of the participants indicated an interest in, or plan to go on to, further training. Implicit in their expression of interest is a desire to do further study from an African centred perspective. The recommendations presented by the focus group participants address both clients and worker concerns.

Recommendations

There were a total of sixty-five recommendations from Halifax, Sydney and the Valley region. This summary identifies those recommendations that tended to be repeated either directly or indirectly.

Most of the recommendations focus on the theme of community networking and communication. There is an emphasis on the need for people in communities to come together to explore and work on issues. There is also an expressed need for individuals and organizations that are urban based to do outreach in the rural regions: for example, sharing information and resources.

Another significant theme was the need to increase the number of African Nova Scotian social workers employed in the rural regions, in child welfare, health, and in clinical social work practice. Recruitment of students to pursue social work as a career and to have more relevant curricula in the social work training program were other key recommendations.

A number of recommendations focused on education: for example, the recruitment of more diverse faculty in higher education institutions; more recruitment of African Nova Scotian students to post secondary education and training; appointed representation on school boards throughout the province; review of adult education curriculum; review of the role and training provided to guidance counsellors and sensitivity training for non-African social workers.

Many of these recommendations focus on ways in which the Nova Scotia Association of Social Workers (NSASW) could have a larger role in the African Nova Scotian community, the relationship between ABSW and NSASW, and the role of ABSW in the community.

There was a recommendation that a separate agency be established for African Nova Scotians, and a suggestion that the Department of Community Services establish a Division similar to the African Canadian Services Division in the Department of Education. Finally, it was recommended that Africentric theory should be made more widely available to community members who might be interested in continuing education in this area.

Although this research was completed in 1998, similar themes and recommendations emerge through the stories told in this book, many of which are based on experiences that happened at a much earlier time. Although not an original goal, the research became part of ABSW's strategy for institutional change in social work education, theory and practice.

References

Akbar, N. (1984). Africentric social sciences for human liberation. *Journal of Black Studies 14*(4), 395-414.

Asante, M.K. (1988). *Africenticity*. Trenton, New Jersey: Africa World Press Ltd.

Asante, M.K. (1987). *The Afrocentric idea*. Philadelphia: Temple University Press.

Asante, M.K. Africentricity. A presentation made in Halifax, Nova Scotia, March 20, 1999.

Bekerie, A. (1994). The four corners of a circle – Afrocentricity as a model of synthesis. *Journal of Black Studies 25*(2), 131-149.

Benton, W. (1997). *The effects of racism on Africans in the diaspora*. Unpublished MSW Thesis. Dalhousie University, Halifax, Nova Scotia.

Bernard, W.T. (1996). *Survival and success: As defined by Black men in Sheffield, England, and Halifax, Canada*. Unpublished Doctoral Thesis. University of Sheffield, Sheffield.

Collins, P.H. (1990). *Black feminist thought*. New York and London: Routledge.

Essed, P. (1991). *Understanding everyday racism: An interdisciplinary theory*. Volume 2 USA: Sage Publications, Inc.

Karenga, M. (1978). *Essays on struggle: position and analysis*. San Diego: Kawaida Publications.

Schiele, J.H. (1994a). Afrocentricity as an alternative world view for equality. *Journal of Progressive Human Services*, 5(1), 5-25.

Schiele, J.H. (1994b). Afrocentricity: Implications for higher education. *Journal Of Black Studies*, 25(2), 150-169

Schiele, J.H. (1996). Afrocentricity: An emerging paradigm in social work practice. *Social Work*, 41(3), 284-295.

Schiele, J.H. (2000). *Human services and the Afrocentric paradigm*. New York, New York: Haworth Press.

Tukufu, D.S. (1997). *A guide toward the development of African males*. Richmond Heights, Ohio: Tukufu.

Chapter 16

Reflections on the Experiences of Fighting for Change

Wanda Thomas Bernard

Introduction

From their modest beginning, to the creation of new pathways, the voices of new students, and the journey to institutional change, these social work trailblazers have told us in their own words, and on their own terms, what their experiences of fighting for change have been. Common threads run through many of the stories by social workers in Section Two and those by social work students in Section Three. The most prominent are: the importance of life experiences in the decision to become social workers as well as in the practice of those who have become social workers; a sense of racial awareness which results in a collective consciousness; and the inadequacy of a Eurocentric approach to meet the needs of people of African descent in social work as is the case with most other aspects of life. Similar themes emerge from the founding members in Chapters 1 and 2. ABSW was organized in Montreal and in Halifax for similar reasons; most significant was the perceived community need and the workers' own sense of community connectedness and responsibility to help effect change in the conditions they witnessed, and in some cases, experienced. The messages of life experience and collective consciousness reappear in Chapter 15, where Bernard, Benton and Baptiste report on their research that explored African Nova Scotian workers' definition of Africentric social work.

Life Experiences as Catalyst

The roots of ABSW in Canada lie in the life experiences of the founding members themselves, and in their early experiences as Black social workers in predominately white societies. Speaking about the founding of ABSW in Montreal, Jacobs says that ABSW formed because of their concerns about the overrepresentation of Black children in care, and the lack of culturally sensitive services. A similar story is told in Chapter 2, where the four founding members of the Halifax chapter of ABSW note that they came together to address concerns they had about the large number of Black foster children who were in white foster homes in isolated communities, and their overall vision of community need. The helping tradition continues in Chapter 3 where Roker writes about the programs and services that ABSW offered in the early years to fill gaps left by the mainstream agencies.

Just like respondents in the exploratory research in Section Four, the participants in Sections Two and Three all attest to the importance of life's experiences in their work. Whether they had been raised within close-knit Black communities, had been wards of the court, adopted by white or Black families other than their biological one, or raised by their own parents who had been single and/or poor, all participants attest to the importance of life's experiences in their choice of work. Some of the contributors, like

Wanda Taylor and Satie Katwaroo Borden, had been in care as children and they allude to how this influenced their career choice. For some participants, early exposure to social services made them aware of inadequacies such as the underrepresentation of Blacks in the social work profession. On the other hand, Satie Katwaroo Borden, who enjoyed the uncommon advantage of having an African Nova Scotian social worker, is unstinting in her appreciation of the importance of having such a role model.

Others, like Maxine Colley Wongus, who had been fostered by family members also confirm the culture of caring and nurturing in the Black community in which they spent their formative years. Many of the contributors, like Wanda Taylor and Erin Desmond, also credits life's experience for their choice of career.

In virtually all the stories, participants see social work as a helping profession. It is easy to discern from the accounts of these women's lives a desire to give something back to the community which had nurtured them. Anne Simmons puts it succinctly when she observes that both her parents and her community gave her a foundation for the helping tradition that she continues today in the social work field. This foundation is similar to the kind of experience which Althea Tolliver, one of the founding members of the Association of Black Social Workers in Nova Scotia, describes in Chapter 2.

It is the same desire to touch the lives of others which propels current students of social work like Erin Desmond and Darlamaine Gero-Hagel toward the profession, whose goal is to effect change. Other participants, like Phyllis Marsh-Jarvis who experienced abuse as an adopted child, see a gap in social work and their choice of a career stems from a need to step in and fill this gap. Similarly, Wanda Taylor underscores the need to continue to value experiences and to use those experiences to transcend the often invisible barriers between social workers and those we work with.

A Sense of Racial Awareness

Participants express a keen sense of racial awareness with respect to their work as well as in their daily lives. In almost all cases, participants report experiencing outright racism very early in life as children in school. For instance in Chapter 4 Lynda Thomas supplies a moving encounter as a young child in elementary school. Such experiences can leave lifelong scares on people, but Lynda and other contributors explain how they were able to resist and survive the everyday racism in their early schooling experiences, to achieve educational success against the odds.

The school system was equally unsparing of biracial children, as Darlamaine Gero-Hagel describes in Chapter 11. In most cases, participants also report a low climate of expectation as teachers and guidance counsellors either put obstacles in their way, as was the case with Anne Simmons, or did not encourage them to go to university. Maxine Colley Wongus bears witness to this poor climate of expectation, and Lois Fairfax attests to the negative effect of this form of neglect. And the problems do not stop at early education. Others like Anne Simmons and Lynda Thomas in Section Two, and current students in Section Three, also recall how they resisted more subtle but equally unsettling forms of racism as students in the university.

While racism by its oppressive nature can be debilitating, participants all demonstrate a coming to consciousness in not only recognizing racism but also in the naming of it as the toxic element it is. The act of deciphering that a teacher who yells at one for offences which would not attract any reprimand for others of a different skin tone is racially motivated (see Wongus, Chapter 7) therefore becomes like a rite of passage which led participants from childhood into a unique womanhood dedicated to resisting racism in all its ramifications. As such, as I state in Chapter 2, from an early age, "I really became aware of issues of race, issues of racism, institutional racism and how it impacted on us. And it was also at that point that I made a decision that I was not going to just be aware of it, but that I was going to do something about it." Lois

Fairfax's account articulates how most participants have managed to turn the adverse effect of racism into strength.

As women of African descent doing social work, they are acutely cognizant that while there is a public avowal of the end of racism, its tentacles continue to hold members of their community hostage. As Black women in a predominantly white profession, they, like the respondents in Section Four, acknowledge "the unconscious decisions and acts that are rooted in a keen awareness of . . . collective experiences and challenges." This translates to a sense of collective consciousness in craving role models who look like them either as fellow students or as co-workers, just as they are mindful of their own positions as role models to others in their community.

Quite apart from the fact that role models inspire, having a person who shares a similar background sometimes serves as a buffer or healing balm. As such, a social work student who senses hostility in a supervisor appreciates being spared the additional horror of having to explain her angst to another authority figure only because she is fortunate to have a person of African descent as her field instructor. Lynda Thomas illustrates this when she writes that she could share her experiences with Joan Mendez, her field instructor, without a lot of explanation, because she knew that she understood. The desire to have role models who look like them and the joy expressed in finally having a Black teacher after so many years of schooling also speaks to issues of collective consciousness, which make participants sensitive to the underrepresentation of Black people as educators.

The theme of collective consciousness played a role in the formation of ABSW as the founders confess that "part of the vision was changing the way social services were being delivered to Black Nova Scotians." It is apparent that in order to achieve this envisioned change, "the face of the School of Social Work" also had to be changed. According to the vision of its founders, one of the motivations for establishing ABSW was because we saw that our needs weren't being met and that as Black women, as Black people, we always need that bond of kinship. We needed it both in our professional lives as well as personal and we just felt that we needed somebody behind us who we could trust and somebody who understood our plight and understood our pain.

It is apparent that this vision has come to fruition in the role which ABSW plays in the lives of Black social workers. It is a place of refuge, where pain can be verbalized, where the sometimes confusing effects of racism, which turn one against oneself in the form of self-doubt, can be unsheathed for what they are. In addition, the contributors, from their vantage positions as members of the Black community, see the connectedness of various facets of life in social work.

Whether they are advocating for their clients, for community service, or offering supports for each other, these workers have a personal and professional commitment to social change. Unsurprisingly, social work students like Darlamaine Gero-Hagel and Tionda Cain see social work as an avenue for working towards social justice. While another current student of social work, Oluronke Taiwo, recognizes that while racial differences may create barriers in social work practice, she holds hope that it can also be a site for decolonization and positive change. In the same vein, Tionda Cain also sees her motivation for studying social work as an expression of her social consciousness. However, as professionals who are also members of a community, they reject the notion of appropriating the voices of others and this is demonstrated by their refusal to speak for all members of their community. Even as students, Lynda Thomas and Maxine Colley Wongus recognized the dangers inherent in purporting to speak for an entire race or to be considered a race expert, and they challenged such expectations.

Contributors also see beyond the statistics to the everyday realities of children and adults who use social services and this allows them to make a distinction between social work, as social change, versus social control. Furthermore, they make a distinction between monetary figures and the needs of the human being. It is not surprising that without exception all participants advocate for the recognition of ABSW as a crucial agent for positive change in the Black community.

Inadequacy of a Eurocentric Approach to Meet the Needs of People of African Descent in Social Work

ABSW initially formed because of vital gaps in social services to African Nova Scotian communities, and this resonates in many of the stories told in this book. As a result of their unique point of view, the implication of race, the pervasive impact of racism, their individual life experiences and collective consciousness, they have a lucid perception and analysis of the interconnectedness and varied forms of oppression and marginalization. Their personal experiences of diverse forms of oppression allow them to empathize with clients and eloquently advocate for them because of their social location and the impact of the intersections of race, disability, economic class and sexual orientation. Essentially, their capacity to fight for change is rooted in their own experiences of racism, resistance and resilience.

This insight also makes them more responsive to the absence of culturally specific services as a significant shortcoming. Katwaroo Borden describes the effectiveness of an Africentric approach to social work and how she has come to rely on it. Lynda Thomas also verbalizes the dangers of cultural alienation and disconnection from community with which a large proportion of service users have to contend due to the failure of the system to adopt other culturally influenced approaches alongside the dominant Eurocentric one.

This is also similar to the perspectives of respondents in Section Four, where they explore Africentric theory, bringing it from the margins to the mainstream. Many of the social workers credit their own resistance and survival in an often hostile and chilly climate to their sense of collective consciousness, positive racial identity and a racialized consciousness. I found similar survival strategies were used by Black men in an earlier study (Bernard 1996). The stories in this book illustrate Africentric theory in action, as it underpins the workers' service to their clients and their communities and underscores the support they give to each other. When they learn to theorize from their location of marginalization and pain (hooks

1993), they transcend those experiences to connect with and advocate for others in similar conditions.

As Roker asserts in Chapter 3, ABSW is at an interesting juncture in its history. This group of committed volunteers have fought for, and experienced change, but how long can they continue to carry the burdens of the Black community, and survive as individual social workers in a racialized and race conscious society? It is my hope that the reading of these stories will help others to carry on the fight for social justice and social change, and help move us to another level of action. And the journey continues as ABSW passes the torch to the next generation.

References

Bernard, W. T. (1996). *Survival and success: As defined by Black men in Sheffield, England, and Halifax, Canada.* Unpublished Doctoral Thesis. University of Sheffield, Sheffield.

hooks, bell. (1993). *Sisters of the yam: Black women and self-recovery.* Toronto: Between the Lines.

Biographies of Contributors

Editor – Wanda Thomas Bernard received a Bachelor of Arts degree from Mount Saint Vincent University, a Master of Social Work from the Maritime School of Social work at Dalhousie University, and a PhD from the University of Sheffield, England. She has worked in mental health at the Nova Scotia Hospital, in rural community practice with the Family Services Association, and since 1990 has been a professor at the Dalhousie School of Social Work, where she has held the position of Director since 2001. She has received numerous awards over the years for her many contributions to social change and social justice in Canada. In 2005 Dr. Thomas Bernard was made a member of the Order of Canada for her work on race and racism in social work and the community at large.

Rene Baptiste has a BSW and MSW from the Dalhousie School of Social Work. She has worked in long-term care, in front-line and management positions. She is currently employed as a consultant in pharmaceutical sales.

Winnie Benton has a BSW and MSW from the Dalhousie School of Social Work. She currently works for the Department of Community Services as a long-term worker in Child Protection, and has worked for the department for eight years. She is also a sessional instructor at the School of Social Work, teaching a graduate course on anti-oppression.

Satie Katwaroo Borden has a BSW and MSW from the Dalhousie School of Social Work. She currently works for the Department of Community Services as a Supervisor of Emergency Duty, and has worked for the department for ten years.

Tionda Cain was born and raised in Toronto. She now lives in Halifax, is studying social work at Dalhousie University and works as a research assistant for the Racism, Violence and Health Project. She holds a BA in Criminology from Simon Fraser University and has worked in the field of violence against women both locally and abroad.

Erin Desmond is currently a BSW student at the Dalhousie School of Social Work. She holds two other degrees, a BA in Sociology from Dalhousie University and a Bachelor of Applied Arts in Family Studies and Gerontology from Mount Saint Vincent University. She now works part-time for the Association of Black Social Workers.

Lois Fairfax is originally from Dartmouth, Nova Scotia, and now lives in Toronto, Ontario. She holds BA, BSW and MSW degrees. She has worked in child welfare for eight years and in children's mental health for seven years. She is presently a social work supervisor in a children's mental health centre outside Toronto.

Darlamaine Gero-Hagel is a second-year MSW student at Dalhousie University. She is currently employed with the Department of Justice as a Family Court Counsellor, Regional Family Justice Services in Red Deer, Alberta, a position she has held for four years, following a twenty-year career in the nursing field. She also sits on the domestic violence steering committee in Red Deer.

Barbara Hamilton-Hinch has a Bachelor of Arts degree, and a Master of Arts in Leisure Studies from Dalhousie University. She is currently a doctoral student in the Interdisciplinary PhD program at Dalhousie and is employed there full-time as the Black Student Advisor.

Diane C. Jacobs is originally from Montreal. She obtained her BA from Concordia University, Montreal; MSW from Howard University, Washington, D.C.; and PhD from Arizona State University, Tempe, Arizona. She currently is Assistant Professor and Director of the Foster Parent Training Program at Tulane University School of Social Work in New Orleans. Diane is one of the founding members of ABSW in Montreal and is responsible for passing the torch to the Halifax group who started ABSW there.

Phyllis Marsh-Jarvis is an undergraduate student at Dalhousie University. She has worked in the human services field for many years, in paid and volunteer capacities. Her many speaking engagements in social work classes address her history of struggle, resistance and survival.

Candace Bernard Roker has a BSW and MSW from the Dalhousie School of Social Work. She also holds an MA in Education from Mount Saint Vincent University. Her MA thesis focused on how the intersection of race, class and gender impacts on school experiences for African Nova Scotian learners. Candace was previously an employee of the Association of Black Social Workers and is currently a social worker at a children's mental health centre in Toronto, Ontario.

Anne Simmons has a Bachelor of Social Work degree from the Maritime School of Social Work at Dalhousie University, and is a registered social worker in the Province of Nova Scotia. Currently she is a social worker with the Children's Aid Society of Halifax, working with children and families in care.

Oluronke Anuoluwapo Taiwo, originally from Nigeria, is now a Canadian citizen and resides in Halifax. She has a BSc in Biology (Ed), an MSc in Medical Microbiology and a diploma in counselling skills. Presently she is a final year BSW student. She works as a house manager in a small options home with mentally challenged clients. She is married with three children.

Wanda L. Taylor, BSW, RSW, is a registered social worker, currently working in the field of child protection as a long-term protection worker in Halifax, Nova Scotia. She is also employed with Phoenix Youth Programs as a relief worker for homeless and at-risk youth between the ages of sixteen and twenty-four, and has worked intermittently in this position for over four years. She is a graduate of the Maritime School of Social Work, Dalhousie University. Wanda is currently involved with several projects promoting women's health and healthy families. She is also writing a non-fiction piece on domestic violence.

Lynda Thomas has a Bachelor of Social Work degree from the Maritime School of Social Work at Dalhousie University, and is a registered social worker in the Province of Nova Scotia. Currently she is the manager of YMCA Enterprise Centre, a community based agency that provides employment and pre-employability related services to the Halifax North community.

Maxine Colley Wongus has a BSW and a Master of Social Work, both from Dalhousie University. She currently works as a health care social worker with Capital District Health, at the Halifax Infirmary Site.

MEMBER OF SCABRINI GROUP

Québec, Canada
2006